ENRICHING FAITH: LESSONS AND ACTIVITIES ON THE BIBLE

※ Enriching Faith ※

LESSONS AND ACTIVITIES ON THE BIBLE

MARY KATHLEEN GLAVICH, SND

TWENTY THIRD 23rd
PUBLICATIONS
www.23rdpublications.com

TWENTY-THIRD PUBLICATIONS
A Division of Bayard
One Montauk Avenue, Suite 200
New London, CT 06320
(860) 437-3012 or (800) 321-0411
www.23rdpublications.com

ISBN: 978-1-62785-027-8
Library of Congress Control Number: 2014935251
Printed in the U.S.A.

CONTENTS

INTRODUCTION

In *The Joy of the Gospel*, Pope Francis wrote, "The study of the sacred Scriptures must be a door opened to every believer. It is essential that the revealed word radically enrich our catechesis and all our efforts to pass on the faith" (175). Even the youngest believers have the right to access the treasures of sacred Scripture. After all, Jesus did say, "Let the little children come to me" (Matthew 19:14).

God's great gift of the Bible shows us who Jesus is: the Son of God and our Savior. It presents salvation history, culminating in the teachings and life of Jesus. It is our story and our children's story. What's more, the Bible is a channel to encounter God, to hear God, and to speak to God.

Unfortunately, for way too long, Catholics lagged behind in knowledge of the Bible. In overreacting to Protestants, who believed only what was in Scripture, the church discouraged Catholics from reading the Bible. We heard Scripture readings at Mass, but these were in Latin. Finally, in 1943, Pope Pius XII, in his encyclical *Divino Afflante Spiritu*, gave impetus to studying the Bible. Catholic biblical scholars flourished. But it wasn't until 1974 that the first Bible-study program for ordinary Catholics in the United States was published (Little Rock Scripture Study). Today many parishes offer some form of Bible study. Understandable versions of the Bible appeared, including in 2013 the first complete Catholic Bible for children from grades one to four (*The Children's Catholic Bible*). Now, with the church's emphasis on new evangelization, familiarity with the Bible has assumed even greater importance.

This Book

The lessons in this book give children keys to unlock Scripture. They learn, not the specific content of the Bible, but rather, basic understandings about it, attitudes toward it, and skills for using it that will make them biblically literate. With this foundation, they will be equipped to explore and mine the riches of the Bible effectively.

For each of the thirty lessons in this book, a one-page plan is provided with one focused objective. Catechist Notes offer background on the topic and also suggest additional ideas for the lesson. Materials needed for the lesson are listed. The steps for developing the topic are few and simple. They engage the children, draw on their experiences, and vary from lesson to lesson. Each lesson is accompanied by an Activity Sheet to be duplicated for the children. The sheets develop or reinforce the lesson in different ways, such as a prayer service, plays, art projects, and paper and pencil activities. A brief prayer concludes the lesson.

Swedish Carmelite Wilfrid Stinissen said, "As a rocket fires off a spaceship outside the earth into space, so the word can propel us into God's endlessness." Several lessons teach how to use the Bible for prayer. This is appropriate, for the ultimate purpose of Scripture is to deepen our relationship with God, a relationship that is nourished by prayer.

By supplementing regular religion lessons with the lessons in this book, teachers, catechists, and parents will bring children closer to praying the prayer of the prophet Jeremiah: "Your words became to me a joy and the delight of my heart" (Jeremiah 15:16).

Important!

The Scripture citations in this book are based on a Bible that begins numbering psalm verses with the psalm itself. Some versions of the Bible, such as THE NEW AMERIAN BIBLE, identify a psalm's introductory information as verse 1. If your children use Bibles where this is the case, the psalm citations for the activities in **Lessons and Activities on the Bible** *will be one verse less than the ones in their Bibles. For example, Psalm 21:1 in this book will be Psalm 21:2 in their Bibles.*

1 THE BIBLE, GOD'S BOOK

Objective

The children will understand that the Bible is holy because it is God's word to us.

Catechist Notes

The Bible is the bestseller of all times for good reason. God is the author! He influenced the writers to record what he wanted. In the Bible, God speaks to us today as really as he spoke to Abraham, Moses, and the people in Israel. There is no blessing for a Bible. It needs none.

Materials

- ☐ **A COPY OF A BESTSELLER LIST** (optional)
- ☐ **A BIBLE** covered with a cloth
- ☐ **A GPS UNIT**
- ☐ **A BOARD OR A LARGE SHEET OF POSTER PAPER AND A MARKER**
- ☐ **PENS OR PENCILS**
- ☐ **COPIES OF ACTIVITY SHEET 1**

Activity

❶ Show a bestseller list, if possible, and discuss:
- Each week, the *New York Times* newspaper publishes a list of bestselling books. Under this cloth is the bestseller of all time. What do you think it is? (the Bible)
- [*Ask a child to uncover the Bible and hand it to you.*]
- Who is your favorite author?
- The Bible is so popular because of its author. There is no author's name on the cover, but who is the author? (God)

❷ Explain inspiration through a story.
- Suppose you broke your arm and had to stay home from school. You wanted to send a letter to your classmates, but you couldn't write. A friend comes over to visit. How could you get your letter written? (The friend could write

it.) Whose letter would it be? (mine)
- This is how God is the author of the Bible. The thoughts are God's, but many different people wrote them for God. God did not dictate the words to them, but he influenced them to write what he wished. We say that God inspired the writers. The Bible is "God-breathed." Inspiration is like mental telepathy.
- Because the Bible is God's book, it has no errors regarding matters of faith.
- How did God speak to Moses? (in a burning bush) To the Israelites? (through prophets) To Mary? (through the Angel Gabriel) To Joseph? (in dreams) God speaks to us in the Bible. God tells us what he is like and how much he loves us. He also tells us how to live so that we will be happy.

❸ On the board or a large sheet of paper write "___ ___ ___ ___ Bible" and "___ ___ ___ ___ ___ ___ Scripture."

Explain that the word *bible* means books and *scripture* means writing. State that we give the Bible two names that indicate that it is God's book. Ask what these names are. (holy, sacred) Have the two children who answer correctly fill in the missing letters.

❹ Distribute copies of Activity Sheet 1 and have the children work it. When they are finished, check Part I. **Answer:** *The Bible is the word of God in the words of human beings.* Then discuss Part II. **Possible answers:** *1. God is the author of the Bible who inspired people to write it for him. 2. Read it. Turn the pages carefully. Cover the Bible. Keep it clean. 3. Don't throw the Bible, put it on the floor, or doodle in it.*

Prayer

Thank you, God, for the gift of your word in Scripture. May reading and listening to it bring me closer to you.

What Is the Bible?

≡ PART ONE ≡

Using the code, write on the lines the letters that match the numbers under the lines. You will see a definition of the Bible.

CODE

A	B	C	D	E	F	G	H	I	J	K	L	M	N	O	P	Q	R	S	T	U	V	W	X	Y	Z
1	2	3	4	5	6	7	8	9	10	11	12	13	14	15	16	17	18	19	20	21	22	23	24	25	26

____ ____ ____   ____ ____ ____ ____ ____   ____ ____
20   8   5   2   9   2   12 5   9   19

____ ____ ____ ____ ____ ____ ____   ____ ____   ____ ____ ____
20   8   5   23 15 18 4   15 6   7   15 4

____ ____ ____ ____ ____   ____ ____ ____ ____ ____
9   14 20 8   5   23 15 18 4   19

____ ____ ____ ____ ____ ____ ____   ____ ____ ____ ____ ____ ____ ____ .
15 6   8   21 13 1   14   2   5   9   14 7   19

≡ PART TWO ≡

1 Use the word *author* and any form of the word *inspire* to explain the meaning of the definition above.

_____

_____

_____

_____

2 If you believe that the Bible is God's word, how will you treat it and handle it?

_____

_____

_____

_____

3 If you believe that the Bible is holy, what won't you do to it?

_____

_____

_____

_____

2 HONORING THE HOLY BIBLE

Objective
The children will learn ways to honor and love God's word, in particular by enthroning the Bible.

Catechist Notes
The Jewish people, our spiritual ancestors, show great esteem for Scripture. Christian monks honored the Bible by painstakingly copying it by hand, creating illuminated manuscripts. By reverently holding the Bible and reading from it in a slow, dignified manner, you will instill in the children respect for God's word.

Materials
- ☐ **An item that is special to you**, *such as a picture of a loved one, a trophy, a homemade gift*
- ☐ **A sample or picture of an illuminated Bible**
- ☐ **A Bible with a page marker set at Matthew 7:24–27**
- ☐ **A prayer table covered by cloth, and on it a crucifix, plant, candle, and matches** *(if allowed; otherwise use an electronic candle)*
- ☐ **Music for the songs chosen for the enthronement**
- ☐ **Copies of Activity Sheet 2**

Activity
❶ Show an item you cherish and tell why it means a lot to you. Explain how you give it special treatment: for example, by displaying it, placing a candle or flowers in front of it, or setting it out on special occasions. Then ask the children to name items they cherish and tell how they treat them.

❷ Explain how Jewish people honor God's word.
- In their places of worship, they keep the scrolls of God's word in a special place in a container called an ark.
- On one of their holy days, they dance with the scrolls of God's word.

❸ Show a sample of an illuminated Bible and comment:
- Before the printing press was invented, monks honored the Bible by spending years producing copies by hand. They printed the words with decorative letters and added illustrations tinted with gold and silver.

❹ Ask how the Bible is honored at Mass. (The Book of the Gospels is carried in the entrance procession and then placed on the altar; it may be incensed; when the presider carries it to the lectern, servers may accompany him with candles; we stand for the gospel; after proclaiming the gospel, the priest or deacon kisses the book.)

❺ State that we can honor the Bible by setting it in a special place during a prayer service called an enthronement. Pass out copies of Activity Sheet 2 and prepare the children for the ceremony:
- Choose a leader to carry the Bible at the head of the procession, place it on the table, bow, and say, "I praise you, God, for your holy word."
- Choose a reader to read from the Bible (or the sheet).
- Designate sides 1 and 2.
- Explain that, in the prayer, God's word is also called the law and ordinances.
- Explain how the procession will go.

❻ Light the candle and carry out the enthronement. Encourage the children to hold an enthronement at home.

Prayer
I praise you, God, for your kindness in giving us your word. May I always read the Bible with reverence and awe.

Enthronement of the Bible

A candle is lit (if fire laws allow).

SONG

A song about God's word, such as "Your Word Is a Lamp unto My Feet"

Leader: O loving God, thank you for the gift of the Bible, which enlightens us. In sacred Scripture we hear the story of your love for us and how you saved us. We learn about you and your teachings. We discover how to live a good life. May we always treasure Scripture and use it to deepen our friendship with you.

All: Amen.

PROCESSION

Carrying a Bible high, a person leads a procession to the prayer table, sets the Bible there, and bows to it, saying, "I praise you, God, for your holy word." Each person approaches the Bible, bows, and repeats the prayer.

READING

Parable of the house built on rock (Matthew 7:24–27)

Everyone then who hears these words of mine and acts on them will be like a wise man who built his house on rock. The rain fell, the floods came, and the winds blew and beat on that house, but it did not fall, because it had been founded on rock. And everyone who hears these words of mine and does not act on them will be like a foolish man who built his house on sand. The rain fell, and the floods came, and the winds blew and beat against that house, and it fell—and great was its fall!

SILENT REFLECTION

How can I give God's word in the Bible a larger role in my life?

PRAYER (from Psalm 119, about the word of God)

Side 1: Happy are those whose way is blameless,

Side 2: who walk in the law of the Lord. (v. 1)

Side 1: How can young people keep their way pure?

Side 2: By guarding it according to your word. (v. 9)

Side 1: I treasure your word in my heart,

Side 2: so that I may not sin against you. (v. 11)

Side 1: Remember your word to your servant,

Side 2: in which you have made me hope. (v. 49)

Side 1: My soul longs for your salvation;

Side 2: I hope in your word. (v. 81)

Side 1: How sweet are your words to my taste,

Side 2: sweeter than honey to my mouth! (v. 103)

Side 1: Your word is a lamp to my feet

Side 2: and a light to my path. (v. 105)

Side 1: The sum of your word is truth;

Side 2: and every one of your righteous ordinances endures forever. (v. 160)

Side 1: I rejoice at your word

Side 2: like one who finds great spoil. (v. 162)

All: Glory be to the Father, and to the Son, and to the Holy Spirit. As it was in the beginning, is now, and ever shall be, world without end. Amen.

3 EXPLORING THE BIBLE

Objective
The children will become familiar with the parts of their Bible, discovering features that help them read and understand it.

Catechist Notes
The books of the Bible were first written on scrolls of papyrus made from the pith of reeds. These were replaced by parchment scrolls made from animal skins. Eventually pieces were bound together to form a codex like our modern books. The printing press made it easier to produce Bibles, but God's word was still inaccessible to the many people who were illiterate. Today when most people can read, Bibles are not only easily obtained, but they include aids for reading them. Having the children examine their Bibles will make them aware of everything that their versions offer. They won't be like the teacher who discovered the reproducible sheets at the back of her manual at the end of the school year!

Beforehand, choose questions in #2 or add questions that correspond to the version of the Bible your children are using.

Materials
☐ **BIBLES**
☐ **A LOCKED CASH BOX OR JEWELRY BOX**
☐ **TREASURE INSIDE THE BOX**, *perhaps a dollar*
☐ **THE KEY TO THE BOX**
☐ **CRAYONS OR MARKERS**
☐ **SCISSORS**
☐ **HOLE PUNCH**
☐ **THIN RIBBON, YARN, OR RAFFIA**
☐ **CLEAR CONTACT PAPER** (optional)
☐ **COPIES OF ACTIVITY SHEET 3** on sturdy paper

Activity
❶ Keeping the key to a locked box hidden, ask for a volunteer to open the box. When the child isn't able to, ask what is needed. (the key) Produce the key and hand it to the child. Comment:

- The word of God is like a treasure, but to enjoy its riches, to understand it, we need the right keys. Today you will search your Bible to find the keys it offers.

❷ From the following questions, ask those that pertain to your children's Bibles.

- Is there a prayer at the front of your Bible, asking for God's help in reading it?
- Does your Bible have an introduction to the whole Bible?
- Are there introductions to each book throughout the Bible?
- What page is the table of contents on?
- Does your Bible tell you the abbreviations of its books?
- Does your Bible have pictures? Maps?
- Does your Bible have footnotes that explain verses?
- For certain verses, does your Bible direct you to related verses?
- At the top of a page do you find book and chapter that are on that page?
- Is there an index in your Bible?
- Does your Bible have a glossary?
- What other helps does your Bible have?

❸ Pass out the copies of Activity Sheet 3 and have the children follow the directions for making bookmarks for their Bibles. They might cover the bookmarks with contact paper.

Prayer
Dear Jesus, as I learn to make my way around the Bible, may it bring me to better know and follow your Way.

A Bible Bookmark

DIRECTIONS

1 Cut out the bookmark and punch a hole in the end.

2 Choose a saying about God's word or create your own. Write it on the bookmark.

Sayings:
» Your word is a lamp for my feet.
» God's word is alive.
» God's word, my treasure.
» God is love.
» Let my word dwell in you. ~Jesus

3 Decorate the bookmark. You might add Christian symbols like the following: a cross, a fish, a sun, a dove, a triangle, a heart, a Bible, a chi rho.

4 String a piece of ribbon, yarn, or raffia through the hole and tie it on.

4 A LIBRARY OF BOOKS

Objective

The children will view the Bible as a collection of books and become acquainted with the names of these books.

Catechist Notes

God chose to convey his message by means of a variety of books gathered into one collection, the Bible. The Jewish people categorized the Old Testament books as belonging to the Law (Torah), the Writings, and the Prophets. The New Testament contains the Gospels, Acts of the Apostles, the Letters, and Revelation. The oldest known biblical manuscripts in existence are among the Dead Sea Scrolls, which were discovered in Qumran by a shepherd in 1947.

You might challenge your children to memorize the biblical books. Here, at least, is a jingle for remembering the first fourteen letters in the New Testament in order to help locate them:

Ro-Co-Co, Gal-Eph-Phi
Col-Thess-Thess, Tim-Tim-Ti
Phil-Heb

Materials

☐ **Bibles**
☐ **Paper**
☐ **Pens or pencils**
☐ **Copies of Activity Sheet 4**

Activity

❶ Form the children into teams. Hold a contest to see which team can list the most kinds of books in a library. Offer biography as an example. After two minutes, ask the team with the longest list to read it. Invite other teams to add to the list.

❷ Show a Bible and compare it to a library.
■ The Bible is like a library because it is composed of many kinds of books. In fact, the word *bible* comes from the

Greek for "the books," which is plural.
■ The books in the Bible belong either to the first part, called the Old Testament, or to the second part, called the New Testament.
■ To find your way around a library, you need to know how the books are grouped. In the Bible, similar books, like the historical books or the Christian letters, are grouped together. In addition, the books are more or less in chronological order.
■ The first five books are called the Pentateuch, which is Greek for five scrolls. Jewish people call them the Torah. They are about the first dealings of God with his people and contain God's law.

❸ Direct the children to turn to their Bible's table of contents. Tell half of the children to count the Old Testament books (46) and the other half to count the New Testament books (27). Then ask how many books there are all together (73).

❹ Distribute copies of Activity Sheet 4. Read the directions and have the children work the sheet.

❺ When the children are finished, check the answers. **Answers:** *1) Genesis; 2) Revelation; 3) Ruth, Esther, Judith; 4) Psalms, Song of Solomon; 5) 1&2 Kings; 1&2 Chronicles; 6) Leviticus; 7) Exodus; 8) Acts of the Apostles; 9) John; 10) Romans; 1& 2 Corinthians, Galatians, Ephesians, Philippians, Colossians, 1&2 Thessalonians; 11) Proverbs, Ecclesiastes, Wisdom, Sirach; 12) Job; 13) Numbers; 14) Matthew, John; 15) Hebrews; 16) 18; 17) Psalms; 18) 3 John; Bonus: Answers will vary.*

Prayer

O God, how creative you are in packaging your word in many forms. May I present your word to others by my words and actions.

Bible Book ID

Use your Bible's table of contents to answer the following questions.

1 What is the first book in the Bible? _____

2 What is the last book? _____

3 Which books are named for women? _____

4 Which books are poetry? _____

5 Which books seem to be historical? _____

6 Which book is about worship and priests from the tribe of Levi? _____

7 In which book does Moses first appear? _____

8 Which book tells the story of Pentecost? _____

9 What is the last gospel? _____

10 Which books are named for people in a city? _____

11 Which books contain adages, sayings for living well? _____

12 Which book is about the mystery of suffering? _____

13 Which book contains a census of the tribes of Israel? _____

14 Which books are named for apostles? _____

15 Which book is named for Jewish Christians? _____

16 How many books by Old Testament prophets are there? _____

17 What is the longest book? _____

18 What is the shortest book? _____

BONUS What book would you be most interested in reading? _____

5 INTERPRETING SCRIPTURE CITATIONS

Objective
Given a Scripture citation, the children will be able to locate the passage it represents.

Catechist Notes
The Bible's chapter divisions were developed about 1227. The Old Testament was divided into verses in 1448. A French printer divided the New Testament into verses in 1551.

When locating a chapter, some children make the mistake of looking for the verse before the chapter number rather than after it. Make sure your children do not do this.

Materials
☐ **BIBLES**
☐ **A GPS OR A MAP**
☐ **A BOARD OR LARGE SHEET OF POSTER PAPER**
☐ **A SLIP OF PAPER** *for each child*
☐ **PENS OR PENCILS**
☐ **A PRIZE** *(optional)*
☐ **COPIES OF ACTIVITY SHEET 5**

Activity
❶ Show a GPS or a map and ask why we use it. (to get to a place) Explain:
- The Bible is a very large book. A system was invented to help us locate any passage in it. It is like a GPS or map. Each Bible book was divided into numbered chapters. These chapters were divided into portions about a sentence long called verses. They too are numbered.
- The breaks between chapters and between verses are not always logical.

❷ Distribute copies of Activity Sheet 5. State that a Scripture citation that directs us to a passage has parts like a house address. Use the diagram on the sheet to explain the meaning of John 3:16. Read the citation for the children: John, chapter 3, verse 16.

❸ Tell the children to locate John 3:16 in their Bibles and read it together.

❹ Give further information about citations and write the examples on the board as you mention them.
- Books with the same name are numbered, for example, 1 Kings and 2 Kings. In a citation this number comes before the name of the book.
- Often only an abbreviation for a book appears in a citation—for example, Gen for Genesis and Jn for John.
- Consecutive verses are connected with a hyphen, as in John 3:16–17. Verses that are separated have a comma between them, as in John 3:16, 21.
- Sometimes after a chapter, a period is used instead of a colon. (John 3.16)
- If the first part of a verse is referred to, it is labeled a. If the second part is referred to, it is labeled b, for example, John 3:16b.

❺ Direct the children to choose a verse at random from the Bible and write its citation on a slip of paper. Tell them to trade papers and locate each other's verses.

❻ Send the children on a hunt through the Bible to discover the answers to the questions on Activity Sheet 5. You might award a prize to the first one to have all correct answers. **ANSWERS**: *1) God; 2) Frogs; 3) Deborah; 4) Donkeys; 5) Cows; 6) Mountains; 7) Salt; 8) Eutychus; 9) 195 or 5 times 39; 10) Lion.*

Prayer
O God, may my searching through the Bible lead me to you.

Finding Your Way Around

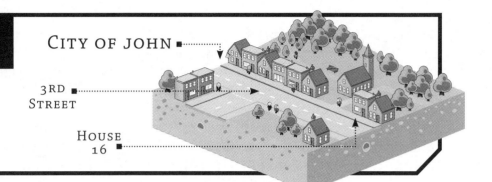

JOHN 3:16

Book [*John*] = city

Chapter [*3*] = street

Verse [*16*] = house number

CITY OF JOHN

3RD STREET

HOUSE 16

Can you answer the following questions?
You can if you locate the verses that the Scripture citations lead you to.

1 Who made clothes for Adam and Eve? (Genesis 3:21) _____

2 What was the second plague God sent to persuade Pharaoh

to let the Israelites go? (Exodus 8:5–6) _____

3 What woman was a judge? (Judges 4:4) _____

4 What was Saul looking for when Samuel anointed him

king of Israel? (1 Samuel 10:2) _____

5 What did Amos call the wealthy women of Israel? (Amos 4:1) _____

6 What does God surround his people like? (Psalm 125:2) _____

7 What did Jesus call his followers? (Matthew 5:13) _____

8 Who fell asleep during Paul's sermon? (Acts 20:9) _____

9 How many times was Paul whipped for being a Christian?

(2 Corinthians 11:24) _____

10 What animal is the devil like? (1 Peter 5:8) _____

6 GOD REVEALS HIMSELF

Objective
The children will identify Scripture as a primary way that God reveals himself to us.

Catechist Notes
God is transcendent, utterly other, nameless, and mystery. We will never fully comprehend God. Creation reflects God. But God took our knowledge of him to a whole new level by entering into our history and interacting with us, beginning with Abraham. God's revelation culminated in Jesus, God made flesh. In Jesus, we see God act and we hear God speak. Scripture is a record of God's actions in BC and AD times. More than that, it is God's words about himself, how God wants us to know him.

Materials
☐ **BIBLES**
☐ **PENCILS OR PENS**
☐ **COPIES OF ACTIVITY SHEET 6**

Activity
❶ Draw a stick figure on the board with four writing lines radiating from it. Tell the children that it is a new classmate. They know nothing about him, not even his name. Ask how they will learn about him and what he is like. Record children's answers on the lines. (People will tell them about him. He will tell about himself. They might read about him somewhere. His actions will reveal what he is like.)

❷ Point out the difficulty of knowing God.
■ God is a pure spirit and invisible. He is so superior to us and so different from us that we can never fully know what God is like.
■ We can draw some conclusions from creation. What can we learn about God from creation? (God must be very intelligent and powerful to make such marvelous things. God must be beautiful and loving.)

■ In general, on our own we don't know much about God.

❸ Explain revelation.
■ Fortunately for us, God has revealed himself. God has interacted with us. God spoke to our ancestors in the faith—for example, to Abraham and Moses. Then God came as a human being, as Jesus, who is the best revelation of God. We know what God is like because we know what Jesus is like.
■ In Scripture we can read about God's saving acts from the beginning of time and learn what he is like. We can read God's very words that reveal him to us.

❹ Distribute copies of Activity Sheet 6. Form small groups and assign each group a passage in a puzzle piece on the sheet. They are to read their passage and write what it reveals about God.

❺ When all are finished, have each group report on its passage and the qualities of God it revealed. Allow children to add qualities. **POSSIBLE ANSWERS:** *Genesis 1:1–3: powerful, good; Exodus 3:7–8: saving; Exodus 34:6: merciful, kind, faithful; Isaiah 6:1–3: holy; Psalm 71:15–16: just, mighty; Psalm 139:1–4: wise, all-knowing; Wisdom 11:21–22: strong, great; John 3:16: loving.*

❻ Explain that the black puzzle piece stands for things about God that we will never understand. They will always be a mystery.

Prayer
God, people can tell who I am and what I'm like by what I say. Your words in Scripture let me know about you. Help me to understand more and more what you are like through them.

What Is God Like?

Look up the Scripture citation and read it. In the puzzle piece write what quality of God it shows.

GENESIS 1:1-3

EXODUS 3:7-8

EXODUS 34:6

ISAIAH 6:1-3

PSALM 71:15-16

PSALM 139:1-4

WISDOM 11:21-22

JOHN 3:16

7 SCRIPTURE AND TRADITION

Objective

The children will understand that Scripture and Tradition form a single deposit of faith.

Catechist Notes

God's self-communication, or revelation, is found in Scripture (both the Old and New Testaments) and Tradition. It is also present preeminently in Jesus, who is the full revelation of God. Jesus entrusted the gospel, the good news of salvation, through the Holy Spirit to the apostles. They spoke about what they learned from Jesus and the Holy Spirit. The apostles' teaching was handed down to bishops and through them from age to age. This living transmission in the church is Tradition. The apostles' message was also recorded in Scripture. The beliefs of the church are enshrined in both Scripture and Tradition.

Materials

☐ **A PICTURE OR A MODEL OF A BIRD THAT FLIES**
☐ **COPIES OF ACTIVITY SHEET 7**

Activity

❶ Show the bird and ask how far it could fly if it had just one wing. (It couldn't fly.) Comment that just as a bird has two wings, we have two sources to know about God. We need both of them.

❷ Ask how we Catholics came to know truths of faith that are not in the Bible. (Some truths have been handed down orally. The church has taught them through her popes and other bishops, the successors of the apostles.)

❸ Explain Tradition:
- Tradition is the living transmission of the gospel entrusted to the apostles through the Holy Spirit.
- Scripture and Tradition together form one deposit of faith. They are the source of all that we believe about God and ourselves. They are like two wings that take us to what God has revealed.

❹ Name some of our beliefs that are not directly contained in the Bible but have come to us through Tradition.
- Mary was free from sin from the first moment of her existence.
- Jesus had no brothers or sisters. Mary was always a virgin.
- Those who die and are not ready for heaven are purified in Purgatory.
- The pope, the bishop of Rome, is the head of the Catholic Church.
- We can pray to saints for help.

❺ Distribute Activity Sheet 7 and use it to lead the children through the development of revelation. Point out how either Scripture or Tradition comes into play in each stage.

Prayer

Jesus, you praised people for their faith. May my faith deepen through my study of both Scripture and Tradition.

The Path of Revelation

God reveals himself as the one God to Abraham.

▽

The stories of God's dealings with his people are passed on orally. (Tradition)

▽

The Jews record in the Old Testament what God revealed to them. (Scripture)

▽

Jesus comes to earth as the full revelation of God.

▽

The apostles teach others about Jesus. (Tradition)

▽

The apostles' teachings are written down. (Scripture)

▽

The church compiles the Old Testament and New
Testament books to form the official Bible. (Tradition)

▽

The apostles' teachings continue to be transmitted through their
successors, the pope and other bishops. (Tradition)

▽

Today Catholics draw the truths of our faith from both Scripture and Tradition.

Tradition   A SINGLE DEPOSIT OF FAITH   **Scripture**

8 THE ROLE OF THE HOLY SPIRIT

Objective

The children will identify the ways that the Holy Spirit is involved with Scripture.

Catechist Notes

The Holy Spirit was the wind that swept over the water at creation. This same Spirit came down on Jesus at his baptism. Jesus promised that the Holy Spirit would be our advocate, our helper. On Pentecost, the Holy Spirit came down on the church. Unfortunately, the Holy Spirit is too often "the forgotten God," an untapped source of power. While we call God the Father the creator, and God the Son the redeemer, we attribute the role of sanctifier to the Holy Spirit. A primary way that the Holy Spirit makes us holy is through Scripture.

If time allows, you might help the children memorize the Prayer to the Holy Spirit. See chapter 22, Memorizing Verses, for methods.

Materials

☐ **BIBLES**
☐ **A CANDLE AND MATCHES** (if fire laws allow; otherwise use an electronic candle)
☐ **BOARD OR POSTER PAPER**
☐ **CRAYONS OR MARKERS**
☐ **SCISSORS**
☐ **COPIES OF ACTIVITY SHEET 8**

Activity

❶ Light the candle. Comment that when power goes out, candles may help us see in the dark.

❷ Read aloud all together the story of Pentecost in Acts of the Apostles 2:1–4. Then ask why fire is a good symbol for the Holy Spirit. (Fire gives light to see, and the Holy Spirit helps us to see truths. Fire is beautiful and mysterious, and so is God. Fire gives warmth, and the Holy Spirit makes us feel safe and peaceful. Fire is a symbol of love and passion, as in "being on fire" for something; and the Holy Spirit helps us burn with love for the word of God.)

❸ Develop the Holy Spirit's connection to Scripture.
- God the Holy Spirit is the Person of the Trinity who is called the sanctifier. To sanctify means to make holy. The Holy Spirit's role is to make us holy. The Holy Spirit's work is related to the Bible in four ways. [Write the number four on the board.]
- First, the Holy Spirit inspired the writers and editors of the Bible. They were instruments in writing what God wanted to make known. The Holy Spirit did not dictate the Bible. Rather, he moved the minds of the human beings.
- Second, the Holy Spirit guided the church to choose the books to include in the Bible as sacred, inspired books.
- Third, the Holy Spirit helps the church interpret the meaning of Scripture passages for us.
- Fourth, the Holy Spirit living within us helps us to understand Scripture as we read or hear it.

❹ Distribute copies of Activity Sheet 8 and ask a child to read the paragraph along the left side.

❺ Encourage the children to pray the Prayer to the Holy Spirit (or just the first two lines) before they read the Bible. Read through the prayer, clarifying its meaning using the explanations at the bottom of the sheet.

❻ Direct the children to create a decorative frame around the prayer. Have them cut out the prayer and keep it in their Bible or memorize it.

Prayer

Holy Spirit, be my companion as I read and reflect on Scripture. Help me to understand it and to live by what you reveal in it.

The Holy Spirit Sheds Light

At the Last Supper, Jesus said, "The Advocate, the Holy Spirit, whom the Father will send in my name, will teach you everything" (John 14:25–26). An advocate is someone who stands by your side and helps you. It is a translation of the Greek word *paraclete.* Other names for the Holy Spirit are gift, counselor, comforter, and friend. The Spirit dwelling within us can help us understand Scripture.

PRAYER BEFORE READING THE BIBLE

Come, Holy Spirit, fill the hearts of your faithful

and kindle in them the fire of your love.

Send forth your spirit and they shall be created

and you shall renew the face of the earth.

Let us pray.

O God, who by the light of the Holy Spirit,

did instruct the hearts of the faithful,

grant that by the same Holy Spirit

we may be truly wise

and ever enjoy his consolations.

Through Christ our Lord. Amen.

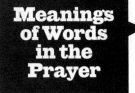

Meanings of Words in the Prayer

Kindle: To start a fire.

Created: The Holy Spirit was present at creation and can create us anew.

Renew: To make good again as God intended.

Wise: To see things as God sees them. To make good decisions.

Consolations: Comfort, feeling of well-being.

THE STORY OF SALVATION HISTORY

9

Objective
The children will understand that the Bible is salvation history, a record of God's saving interactions with the human race.

Catechist Notes
Unlike secular history, salvation history focuses on our relationship with God and his saving acts on our behalf from our creation to the end of time. It culminates in Jesus Christ, God made human. His death and resurrection redeemed us, saved us from sin and death, and won eternal life for us. The end of the apostolic age, namely, the death of the last apostle, marks the end of salvation history as recorded in the Bible. The Bible is not intended to be strict history or a science book, but the faith story of a people. As Galileo remarked, its purpose is not to teach how the heavens go, but how to go to heaven.

Materials
- ☐ **A HISTORY BOOK**
- ☐ **A BIBLE**
- ☐ **PENS OR PENCILS**
- ☐ **COPIES OF ACTIVITY SHEET 9**

Activity
❶ Show the history book and ask the children to name some people and events they would expect to find in the book.

❷ Hold up the Bible and explain salvation history.
- The Bible contains a special kind of history called salvation history. Like a history book, the Bible is about important people and events in the past. But they are all connected with God's saving acts. The word *salvation* comes from the word *save*. The Bible tells the story of God's relationship with us.
- Salvation history begins with our creation and God's promise to save us.

It is about how God revealed himself to the Israelites. It is a record of how God gave his chosen people his law, saved them over and over, and forgave them.
- Salvation history reached its highpoint when God became a human being and saved us by dying and rising. This is so significant that all time is referred to as BC (before Christ) and AD (after Christ). AD is the initials of *anno Domini*, which is the Latin for "year of the Lord."
- Salvation history lasts until the end of time, so we are part of it.

❸ Explain how salvation history differs from secular history.
- In a history book, you find facts and truths. The Bible is not strictly a history book. It does contain some facts, but it is chiefly a book of faith. The Bible's truths about God are sometimes presented through fictional stories and poetry and prophecies filled with symbolic happenings.

❹ Distribute copies of Activity Sheet 9. Tell the children that they are familiar with much of salvation history. Instruct them to use their knowledge to complete the timeline on the activity sheet. You might have the children work in pairs.

❺ After the children have finished working Activity Sheet 9, correct it with them. Elaborate on any of the items as you see fit. **ANSWERS:** *Adam, Abraham, Moses, Joshua, Judges, David, Solomon, Israel, temple, Greece, Romans, church*

Prayer
Dear God, you are so good to care about us, the people you made. Over and over in our history you show your love, forgive us, and act to bring us to live with you. Make me more worthy of being with you forever.

Salvation History
THE STORY OF GOD'S SAVING ACTIONS

Complete the timeline by completing the missing words. (c. means about.)

BC

? God creates A_____ and Eve.

c. 1850 God makes a covenant with A_____ and promises a Savior.

c. 1700 The Israelites move to E_____ and become slaves.

c. 1280 M_____ leads the Exodus from Egypt.

c. 1250–1200 J_____ leads the people into the Promised Land.

c. 1200–1020 J_____ rule the twelve tribes of Israel.

c. 1020–961 King D_____ creates the kingdom of Israel.

961–922 King S_____ builds the Jerusalem Temple.

922 The Kingdom splits in two: Israel in the north, Judah in the south.

721 Assyria conquers I_____ and deports its people.

621 King Josiah reforms Judah's religion.

587 Babylon destroys Jerusalem, and the Jews in Judah are exiled.

538–515 The Jews return to Jerusalem and rebuild the T_____.

c. 333 Alexander captures Jerusalem for his country, G_____,

197–142 Syria rules Judah, and its king persecutes the Jews.

164 The Jewish Maccabees revolt and win Judah's independence.

63 The R_____ conquer Judah.

c. 4 Jesus the Savior is born.

c. 33 The Holy Spirit comes to the C_____ on Pentecost.

AD

THE RELATIONSHIP BETWEEN THE TESTAMENTS

Objective

The children will understand that the New Testament lies hidden in the Old Testament, and the Old Testament is unveiled in the New Testament.

Catechist Notes

The Old Testament and New Testament are equally inspired and important. Knowledge of the Old Tetament helps us understand the meaning of New Testament themes such as sacrifice, covenant, and Messiah. Both Testaments reveal God's love. The people, events, and objects in the Old Testament point to the fulfillment of God's promises with the coming of Jesus Christ.

Materials

☐ **BIBLES**
☐ **PENS OR PENCILS**
☐ **COPIES OF ACTIVITY SHEET 10**

Activity

❶ Distribute copies of Activity Sheet 10 and direct the children to work the activity at the top of the page. The word formed by the combined lines is *Jesus*. Tell the children that the name Jesus means "God saves."

❷ Explain how the Old Testament and New Testament mesh to present the good news of Jesus, the Savior.

■ The Bible has two parts, the Old Testament and the New Testament. The word *testament* means covenant, an agreement. The Old Testament is about God's covenant with the chosen people, the Israelites. The New Testament is about the new covenant established by Jesus.

■ Both the Old Testament and the New Testament are important. They both contain God's revelation and the story of his saving love.

■ Just as the lines in the puzzle merge to reveal Jesus, the Old Testament and New Testament present Jesus. In the Old Testament are people, events, and objects that foreshadow, or hint at, Jesus and New Testament happenings. These hints are called types or figures. We say that they prefigure, or foreshadow, what is in the New Testament.

❸ Name the following types and ask the children to state what they prefigure in the New Testament.

» Isaac, Abraham's son, carries the wood up the hill where he is to be sacrificed. (Jesus, God's only Son, carries his cross to the hill of Calvary.)

» Joseph is sold by his brothers for twenty pieces of silver. (Jesus is turned over to the chief priests by the apostle Judas for thirty pieces of silver.)

» The blood of a sacrificed lamb applied to doorposts protects the Hebrews from death in Egypt. (The blood of Jesus on the cross saves us from death.)

» Manna, bread from heaven, feeds the Israelites on their journey to the promised land. (The Eucharist fills us with divine life on our way to heaven.)

❹ State that the Old Testament also contains prophecies about the Messiah. Read aloud the first paragraph under Part II.

❺ Instruct the children to work the rest of Activity Sheet 10. **ANSWERS:** *1) C; 2) J; 3) E; 4) I; 5) B; 6) G; 7) A; 8) H; 9) D; 10) F.*

Prayer

Jesus, the Old Testament points to you. May my words and example point others to you too. May they see you in me.

TWO TESTAMENTS, ONE MESSAGE
God Saves

≡ PART ONE ≡

Imagine that the bottom window is placed over the top one. Draw the horizontal lines over the vertical ones where they would be. What do they spell?

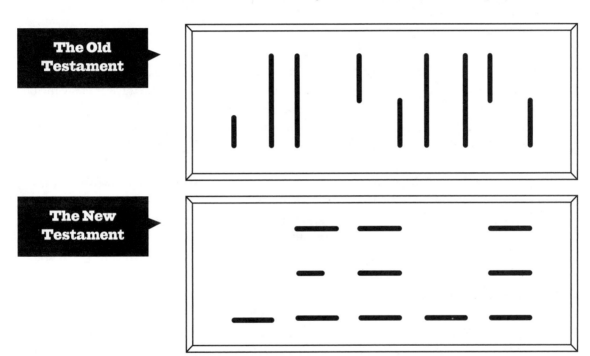

The Old Testament

The New Testament

≡ PART TWO ≡

After his resurrection, Jesus appeared to his disciples and helped them understand how what was written about him in the Old Testament was fulfilled. (See Luke 24:44–48.)

Look up the Scripture citation and find what it prophesies about the Messiah in Column 2. Write the letter of the prophecy on the line.

COLUMN 1

____ 1 Genesis 49:10

____ 2. Micah 5:1–2

____ 3. Jeremiah 23:5

____ 4. Isaiah 7:14

____ 5. Isaiah 35:5–6

____ 6. Isaiah 53:1–3

____ 7. Zechariah 12:10

____ 8. Psalm 22:18–19

____ 9. Psalm 34:20–21

____ 10. Psalm 16:10

COLUMN 2

A. He would be pierced.

B. He would cure people.

C. He would be of the tribe of Judah.

D. His bones would not be broken.

E. He would be descended from King David.

F. He would rise from the dead.

G. He would be rejected.

H. Men would gamble for his garments.

I. He would be Immanuel (God with us).

J. He would be born in Bethlehem.

11 THE BIBLE AS LOVE LETTER

Objective

The children will know that in the Bible God speaks to them personally, and they will experience the Bible as God's love letter to them.

Catechist Notes

The Bible is a vehicle for God to speak to each person's heart. Sometimes a verse or a passage strikes home, and we just know that God intended it for us. The primary message God sends us in Scripture is "I love you." The title of Eugene Boylan's book *This Tremendous Lover* is an apt name for God. The incredible love God has for us is revealed in the Bible in his deeds recounted there as well as in his words.

For an enrichment activity, you might write appropriate Scripture verses on slips of paper and place them in a Valentine candy box (or in fortune cookies, Bugle snacks, or a "mailbag"). Then invite the children to take one and read it as God's personal message for them that day.

Materials
- ☐ **BIBLES**
- ☐ **BOARD OR LARGE POSTER PAPER AND MARKERS**
- ☐ **THESE SCRIPTURE CITATIONS DISPLAYED:**
  Isaiah 43:1–4 • Isaiah 49:15 • Isaiah 54:10 Jeremiah 31:3 • John 15:9
- ☐ **PENS OR PENCILS**
- ☐ **RECORDED SONG ABOUT GOD'S LOVE**
- ☐ **CD PLAYER**
- ☐ **COPIES OF ACTIVITY SHEET 11**

Activity

❶ Draw a large heart on the board with five rays emanating from it. Ask why we exchange Valentine cards. (to let someone know we love them)

❷ Develop the concept that in the Bible God reveals his love for us.

- The Bible is like a giant Valentine from God to us. In fact, it is like a very long love letter. Someone once said that the Bible is a book drenched in love.
- You might know the song that begins "Jesus Loves Me. This I know, for the Bible tells me so."
- In the Bible, God shows us his love over and over.

❸ Ask the children to name God's deeds in the Bible that show his love. Record each answer on a line coming from the heart. (Answers may include creating us, sharing his life, becoming human, dying for us, teaching us, giving us Mary as a mother, staying with us in the Eucharist.)

❹ Explain that God wants us to take his words in the Bible personally. He speaks directly to us about our present circumstances and about our relationship with him. Often God declares his love for us and assures us that he is there with us, loving us and saving us.

❺ Assign groups of children each a Scripture citation to look up, a "love note" from God from the displayed list. Call on children to read each love note. After each one is read, reread it, inserting the names of some children after the word *you*.

❻ Distribute Activity Sheet 11 and instruct the children to complete it. As they work, play a song about God's love. **ANSWER:** *"Scripture enables us to know the heart of God through the word of God."*

Prayer

Jesus, may your words touch my heart. May I always respond to your love with love.

God Loves Me!

≡ PART ONE ≡

Complete this quotation by crossing out every C, I, S, and V
and writing the remaining letters on the lines.

C I K V S N I V C O S W T C V I H C E H I C E V A S R S C T I O V F G S O C I D T V S

H R C O I U V S G I H C T S V H C E W I R S C O S I R V C I D S O I F V G I C O S D

"Scripture enables us to __ __ __ __   __ __ __   __ __ __ __ __

__ __   __ __ __   __ __ __ __ __ __   __ __ __

__ __ __ __ __   __ __   __ __ __ __ . "   SAINT GREGORY THE GREAT

≡ PART TWO ≡
Write a love
letter back
to God.

12 TYPES OF WRITING

Objective
The children will realize that the truths in the Bible are conveyed through different literary styles.

Catechist Notes
The Bible is a mosaic of books that are of many different styles. There are short stories, historical accounts, prophetic books, letters, and even a love song in God's book. Some books are fiction; others are nonfiction. Some are poetry; others are prose. In 1943, Pope Pius XII issued a groundbreaking encyclical, *Divino Afflante Spiritu*. In it he encouraged Scripture scholars to explore how literary styles impact the interpretation of Scripture. This meant that we are not always to take the Bible literally.

Materials
☐ **Pens or pencils**
☐ **Copies of Activity Sheet 12**

Activity
❶ Illustrate the importance of identifying genres by telling about Orson Welles and his infamous radio broadcast.
- In 1938, during a radio broadcast, a man named Orson Welles told the story of a novel called *War of the Worlds*. This book is about Martians invading Earth. For an hour, Welles presented the story in the form of news bulletins. People tuning in late missed the introduction and thought that aliens really were attacking us. There was widespread panic.
- On the other hand, people who heard the radio program introduced as a fiction story weren't fooled.

❷ Tell the children to suppose that they wish to write something to convey the message that bullying is wrong and harmful. Ask what form of writing they might choose. As an example, suggest writing a play. (Answers could include an interview, a short story, a poem, a report, a letter.)

❸ Explain that there are literary styles in the Bible.
- God chose different styles of writing, or genres, to deliver his messages to us. In order to uncover the truth that God is revealing, we need to know characteristics of these styles.
- In Genesis, God punishes the snake by having him crawl on the ground. How did the snake get around before? This is puzzling unless you know that the Jewish people told about the Fall in the form of a story to convey the basic truths about it.
- In the book the Song of Solomon, a man says to his bride, "Your hair is like a flock of goats" and "Your teeth are like a flock of shorn ewes." This sounds very strange unless you know that the book is poetry.
- The Book of Revelation tells of armed locusts with human faces, beasts, and a dragon. It can be frightening unless you know that it is written in a literary style characterized by symbols.
- In some books there is more than one literary style. For example, a story might include a poem.

❹ Distribute Activity Sheet 11. Read, or have children read aloud, the description of each style of writing found in parentheses.

❺ Have the children read the directions and work the activity. Check their answers. **Answers:** *1) D; 2) A; 3) G; 4) F; 5) B; 6) C; 7) E.*

Prayer
How sweet are your words to my taste, sweeter than honey to my mouth! (**Psalm 119:103**)

Writing Samples from God's Book

For each writing style below, an example from the Bible is given. Match the example with the truth it conveys by writing the letter of the truth on the line.

1. **Story** (*an account of an event, fiction or nonfiction*)
_____ God sent the prophet Jonah to tell a town to repent. The people and even the livestock wear sackcloth and ashes as a sign of repentance. God forgives them.

2. **Poem** (*writing with repetition, rhythm, and much figurative language*)
_____ In Psalm 104 God makes the clouds his chariot and rides on the wings of the wind.

3. **Prophecy** (*predictions, often through visions*)
_____ The prophet Ezekiel saw a valley full of dry bones. The bones came together and were covered with flesh. The men came to life and stood up.

4. **Apocalyptic Literature** (*prophecy symbolically teaching God's triumph in the end*)
_____ In a vision John saw an angel pour a bowl on the throne of a beast. Darkness fell, and people in that kingdom who did not repent suffered pain and sores.

5. **Proverb** (*a wise saying*)
_____ Like a gold ring or an ornament is a wise rebuke to a listening ear. (Proverbs 25:12)

6. **History** (*a factual account of a past event*)
_____ The young shepherd David believed that God would help him in battle. Armed with only a slingshot, he dared to fight a huge soldier. David killed him, and the enemy army fled.

7. **Letter** (*a written message to a person or persons*)
_____ Paul encourages the Corinthians to donate and not reluctantly, because God loves a cheerful giver. (2 Corinthians 9:7)

A. God is almighty, majestic, and speedy.

B. A scolding can be helpful.

C. Trusting in God enables us to do the impossible.

D. God is merciful.

E. We should be happy to give to the needy.

F. Eventually evil people will be punished.

G. God will bring people back to life.

13 HOW THE BIBLE WAS COMPILED

Objective
The children will learn how the Bible was formed over centuries and be able to define terms related to the biblical canon.

Catechist Notes
The Catholic Bible combines Hebrew books and Christian writings. Jews and Christians alike did not always agree on which books were divinely inspired and worthy of a place in the canon. Today Protestant Bibles have sixty-six books, while Catholic Bibles have seventy-three.

The terms in this lesson are difficult, but children, who pride themselves on knowing the names of dinosaurs, will consider it a welcome challenge. The independent study activity is a quick, easy way to teach these terms and results in self-satisfaction.

Materials
- ☐ **TERMS ON THE BOARD OR LARGE POSTER PAPER:** *canon, Septuagint, Vulgate, apocryphal, deuterocanonical*
- ☐ **A SHEET OF PAPER FOR EACH CHILD** *to use as a cover sheet*
- ☐ **PENS OR PENCILS**
- ☐ **COPIES OF ACTIVITY SHEET 13**

Activity
❶ State that when families get together, they often tell stories about themselves and their ancestors. Maybe they tell how Mom and Dad met or how Uncle Joe won the lottery. Share one of your family stories. Then invite the children to add theirs.

❷ Present how the Bible evolved.
- God's people, the Israelites, too, told family stories. Some were about their relationship with God. Sometimes they wrote songs about key events. This was how the Bible began—oral accounts.
- What would a family do if they wanted a permanent record of its stories?

(record them, write them down)
- The Israelites eventually recorded their stories on scrolls. Some stories were different versions of the same event. In time these stories were combined, edited, and accepted as sacred Scripture.
- The same process was true for the gospels. Stories about Jesus were told and then written down.
- The church, with the help of the Holy Spirit, decided which books were inspired by God and should be part of the Bible.

❸ Explain that the displayed words are related to the forming of the Bible. Read them aloud. Tell the children that they will teach themselves the meaning of these words. They will also find out how Catholic and Protestant Bibles are different.

❹ Distribute copies of Activity Sheet 13 and give these directions:
- Place the cover sheet over the activity sheet. You will move it down to reveal one frame at a time. Each frame has a piece of information. Most of them end with a question you are to answer. When you move the cover sheet to the next frame, the answer is revealed and you can see if you were right.
- When you reach the bottom of the sheet, you will know the meanings of the words on the board.

❺ When the children have finished working the sheet, ask them to define the words on the board.

Prayer
The prophet Jeremiah claimed that when he found God's words, he devoured them. He prayed, "Your words became to me a joy and the delight of my heart." O God, may I too devour your words.

Putting Together the Bible

Cover the frames. Move the cover sheet down to reveal one frame at a time.
Read the frame and answer its question. Move down to the next frame to see the answer.

The canon of the Bible is the official list of divinely inspired books. This is how it came about.

The Jews wrote down their oral stories and traditions. In 400 BC, they compiled their books of the Law, the prophets, and writings. In the third century BC, this Bible was translated into Greek. This version, called the Septuagint, was used by the early Christians.

Jewish rabbis fixed the Hebrew canon in about 98 AD. They rejected seven books that were in the Septuagint, perhaps because they were too recent. Protestants adopted this shorter Hebrew Bible instead of the Septuagint. They call the seven books the Apocrypha.

Q: What is the canon?

A:
Official list of divinely inspired books

The Apocrypha are Judith, Tobit, Wisdom, Ecclesiasticus, Baruch, and 1, 2 Maccabees. (You can remember them by recalling the initials of a fictional wild-west gang: J.T. Web and the 2 McCabes.) Catholics accept these books as inspired but call them deuterocanonical, which means secondary canon.

Q: What is the Greek version of the Old Testament?

A:
Septuagint

In the first century AD, letters and a number of gospels were written. Variations of the canon were proposed. The New Testament books as we know them were identified by St. Athanasius in 367 AD. The gospels and other Christian books that did not become part of the New Testament canon are called Apocrypha.

Q: What do Protestants call the seven books not included in their Bible?

A:
Apocrypha

In 382 AD, St. Jerome translated the Bible from Greek into Latin, which was the language of the people. His translation is known as the Vulgate.

Q: What do Catholics call the Old Testament Apocrypha?

A:
Deuterocanonical

In 1546, at the Council of Trent, the canon of the Bible was finally set.

Q: What is St. Jerome's Bible called?

A:
Vulgate

14 WHAT THE BIBLE SAYS ABOUT ITSELF

Objective

The children will understand more about the Bible from what the Bible says about God's word.

Catechist Notes

The parable of the sower is a lengthy lesson on God's word found in Matthew, Mark, and Luke. After telling the parable, Jesus, uncharacteristically, explains its meaning. (See Matthew 13:1–23.) The fates of seeds in different environments correspond to the fate of God's words in people's lives. In the parable, much seed is wasted, but what does grow produces a great amount, in fact, an impossible amount!

Acting out the parable of the sower is fun for children. They might perform the play for their parents. As an additional activity, they could draw pictures or create a mural of the parable of the sower.

Materials

- [ ] **BIBLE**
- [ ] **HIGHLIGHTER**
- [ ] **SCRIPTURE VERSES ON SLIPS OF PAPER**
  and inserted in different places in the Bible:
  - The grass withers, the flower fades; but the word of our God stands forever. Isaiah 40:8
  - Like rain and snow bring forth plants, God's word has results. Isaiah 55:10–11
  - Is not my word like fire, says the Lord, and like a hammer that breaks a rock in pieces? Jeremiah 23:29
  - One does not live by bread alone, but by every word that comes out of the mouth of God. Matthew 4:4
  - Whatever was written in former days was written for our instruction, so that by the encouragement of the scriptures we might have hope. Romans 15:4
  - The word of God is living and active and sharper than any two-edged sword. Hebrews 4:12
  - You accepted the word of God not as a human word but as God's word, which is at work in you believers. 1 Thessalonians 2:13

- [ ] **COPIES OF ACTIVITY SHEET 14** *with the children's parts highlighted*
- [ ] **PROPS FOR THE PLAY** *on Activity Sheet 14*

Activity

❶ State that God reveals things about his word in the Bible. Offer the example of how one day when someone praised Jesus' mother, Jesus said, "Blessed rather are those who hear the word of God and obey it!" (Luke 11:28). Clarify that this wasn't a putdown of Mary. She certainly heard the word of God and obeyed it more than anyone.

❷ Call on children to draw a slip from the Bible and read it aloud. After each passage is read, ask the class what they think it means.

❸ Ask for volunteers for parts in the play on Activity Sheet 14. As they volunteer, give them their highlighted sheet. The rest of the class can be the crowd.

❹ Go through the script, directing the children where to stand and how to move.

❺ Have the children perform the play.

❻ Review the meaning of the parable of the sower (as Jesus explained) by asking:
  - How is what happened to the four groups of seeds what happens to God's word in people?

Prayer

"Your word is a lamp to my feet, and a light to my path" (PSALM 119:105). I thank you, God, for guiding me.

The Sower: A Play

> ✪ **CAST:** Jesus, Farmer, Two Seeds for path, Two Seeds for rocks, Two Seeds for thorns, Three Good Seeds, Two Birds, Two Thorns, Sun, Crowd
>
> ✪ **PROPS:** Flashlight for sun, Nineteen paper ears of corn, Basket

(Jesus and Crowd are at the side. Thorns are stooping. Farmer and Seeds are offstage. Good Seeds hold three, six, and ten ears of corn respectively.)

Jesus *(to Crowd)*: One day a farmer went out to sow some seeds.
(Farmer and Seeds enter. He flings the Seeds to their places. The Seeds stoop. Farmer exits.)

Jesus *(pointing to Seeds on path)*:
Some seeds fell on the path and were trampled on. Birds came and ate them.
(Birds fly in, take away Seeds on path.)

Jesus *(pointing to Seeds on rocky ground)*: Other seeds fell on rocky ground where they had little soil and water. They sprang up right away.
(Two Seeds stand.)

But as soon as the sun came up . . .
(Sun shines.)

they were scorched and, not having roots, they withered away.
(Seeds sink to ground.)

Jesus *(pointing to Seeds in thorns)*:
Other seeds fell among thorns. The thorns grew up and choked them, and they produced no crops.
(Thorns and Seeds rise. Thorns wind arms around Seeds' necks. Seeds fall.)

Jesus *(pointing to Good Seeds)*: Other seeds fell on rich soil and, growing tall and strong, produced their crop.
(Good Seeds stand, smile, and flex arms.)

Some thirty.
(One Good Seed holds out three ears.)

Some sixty.
(One Good Seed holds out six ears.)

Even a hundredfold.
(One Good Seed holds out ten ears. Farmer returns with basket and gathers corn from Good Seeds.)

Jesus: Listen, anyone who has ears. The seed is the word of God. The seed on the path *(walks to path, points to it)* are people who hear the word, but Satan takes it from their hearts.

   Those who received the seed on rocky ground *(moves to rocky ground)* first hear the word with joy and believe for a while. But they have no roots. If a trial comes or persecution because of the word, they fall away.

   Then there are those who receive the word in thorns. *(Moves to Thorns.)* These heard the word, but the worries, riches, and pleasures of life choke the word, so they produce nothing.

   (Moves to Good Seeds.) And there are those who received the seed in rich soil. They hear the word and accept it and yield a harvest thirty, sixty, and a hundredfold.

15 THE BIBLE AND THE CHURCH

Objective
The children will understand that the Bible is the church's story and that the church decided what books would be in the Bible, interprets them, and uses them in worship and prayer.

Catechist Notes
Theologian Karl Rahner commented, "The Bible is in the church, not above it." Some religious denominations are known as people of the book. Catholics are not, because our faith is based on both Scripture and Tradition. Nevertheless, the Bible is intimately connected to the church historically and now. The church drew up the canon and has the power to interpret the Bible. As St. Augustine taught, "We must read the Scriptures seated in the lap of our mother the church." Moreover, God's word plays a major role in our worship.

Materials
☐ **BIBLES**
☐ **A CLEAR GLASS OR JAR** *containing water*
☐ **FOOD COLORING, TEMPERA PAINT, OR WATERCOLOR PAINT**
☐ **A SPOON**
☐ **PENS OR PENCILS**
☐ **FLASHCARDS:** *Canon, Interpretation, Worship, Story*
☐ **COPIES OF ACTIVITY SHEET 15**

Activity
❶ Call on a child to add a drop of coloring to water. Then ask the child to separate the coloring from the water. When the child replies that this is impossible, comment:
- Just as the color and the water are united, God's word and the church are inseparable.

❷ Display the first three flashcards one by one and explain how they are ways that the church and the Bible are related:

- [Canon] The canon is the official list of books considered divinely inspired. It was the church who decided which books were to be included.
- [Interpretation] The Holy Spirit helps the church interpret passages in the Bible. For example, at the Last Supper, Jesus said, "This is my body" and "This is my blood." Some people think Jesus was speaking figuratively. The church, however, tells us that Jesus really meant that bread and wine become his body and blood.
- [Worship] The church uses Scripture in the celebration of the Eucharist and other sacraments; in the Divine Office, its official daily prayer; and in personal prayer.

❸ Ask the children what their biography would include. (Family members, ancestors, nationality, characteristics, experiences)

❹ Show the flashcard "Story" and comment:
- The Bible is like the biography of the church. It is our story.

❺ Distribute copies of Activity Sheet 15. Read the directions and have the children work the sheet. They might work with partners.

❸ Correct the Activity Sheet. **ANSWERS:** *1) I; 2) E; 3) F; 4) H; 5) A; 6) D; 7) J; 8) G; 9) B; 10) C. A: Mary; B: Jesus; C: Abraham, Isaac, Jacob; D: Beatitudes; E: Lord's Prayer; F: Father's house (heaven); G: Commandments; H: God made us; I: Scripture; J: Stephen.*

Prayer
O loving God, plant in me the desire to learn more about you and myself by reading your words in Scripture.

The Bible: The Church's Story

Under "Story Facts" are topics belonging to the church's story.
Look up each Scripture reference. On the line before it, write the letter of the topic under "Story Facts" that it reveals. Then on the line below the topic, identify what is named.

Scripture References

1. _____ 2 Timothy 3:16–17

2. _____ Matthew 6:9–13

3. _____ John 14:2

4. _____ Genesis 1:27

5. _____ John 19:26–27

6. _____ Matthew 5:3–11

7. _____ Acts 7:59–60

8. _____ Deuteronomy 5:6–21

9. _____ Matthew 16:18

10. _____ Exodus 4:5

Story Facts

A. Our mother

_____

B. Our founder

_____

C. Our Jewish ancestors

_____

D. Our code of behavior

_____

E. Our prayer

_____

F. Our destiny

_____

G. Our laws

_____

H. Our origin

_____

I. Our book for how to live

_____

J. Our first martyr

_____

16 SCRIPTURE IN THE MASS

Objective
The children will realize that at Mass they feast at the table both of the word and of the Eucharist.

Catechist Notes
The worship in the Jewish synagogue of Jesus' time was centered on Scripture—the praying of psalms, a reading from Scripture, and then a commentary on the reading. Our Eucharist follows this pattern. During the Liturgy of the Word we listen to readings from Scripture. Then these are explained and applied to our lives in a homily. After having nourished our minds and hearts at the table of the word, we partake of the sacred bread and wine.

If time allows, in step number 3 you might read the entire Emmaus story from Luke 24:13–35 instead of the short version on Activity Sheet 16.

Materials
- ☐ **BIBLES** *for half the class*
- ☐ **TWO SETS OF CARDS ON DIFFERENT COLORED PAPER.** *(Duplicate the matching pairs according to the number of children. Note that two copies of "Holy, Holy" are required.)*

    [SET 1]
    Lord, have mercy • Gloria • Holy, Holy • Holy, Holy • Our Father • Lamb of God • Lord, I am not worthy

    [SET 2]
    Psalm 123:3 • Luke 2:14 • Matthew 21:9 • Isaiah 6:3 • Matthew 6:9–13 • John 1:29 • Luke 7:6–7
- ☐ **PENS OR PENCILS**
- ☐ **COPIES OF ACTIVITY SHEET 16**

Activity
❶ Explain that several of our Mass prayers are rooted in Scripture. Give each child one of the prepared cards. Direct those with the Scripture citations to look up their passage. Instruct the children to find the partner who holds the card that matches theirs. Inform them that there are two (or more) Scripture citations for the Holy, Holy.

❷ After all the cards are matched, read each prayer and call on a child who has the matching Scripture verse to read it.

❸ Distribute copies of Activity Sheet 16. Have two children each read a paragraph of "Recognizing Jesus," an abbreviated account of the disciples on the way to Emmaus.

❹ Develop the two ways Jesus is known.
- By what two ways did the disciples come to know Jesus that day? (He explained Scripture to them. He joined them in the breaking of the bread.)
- Today we come to know Jesus in the same two ways during Mass. We celebrate the Liturgy of the Word in which we learn about Jesus and hear him speak to us. Then we celebrate the Liturgy of the Eucharist when Jesus comes to us under the forms of bread and wine.
- At Mass, we are fed in two ways. We feast on the word of God during the Liturgy of the Word. Then during the Liturgy of the Eucharist we feast on Jesus, who, by the way, is called the Word of God.

❺ Have the children work the activity at the bottom of Activity Sheet 16. Then correct their answers. **ANSWERS:** *1) 7; 2) 3; 3) 1; 4) 8; 5) 6; 6) 4; 7) 2; 8) 5.*

Prayer
Jesus, may your words be in my mind, on my lips, and in my heart.

The Table of the Word

THE LITURGY OF THE WORD

Recognizing Jesus

(ADAPTED FROM LUKE 24:13–35)

On Easter Sunday, two disciples left Jerusalem and were going to the village of Emmaus. They were sad as they talked about Jesus. They had hoped that Jesus was the Messiah, but he had been crucified. Jesus joined them. However, the disciples didn't recognize him. They told the stranger what they were saying. He scolded them for not believing in what prophets said about the Messiah having to suffer. Then Jesus explained what Scripture had said about him. When they came near Emmaus, it was late in the day. The disciples invited their mysterious companion to stay with them.

As they ate, Jesus took bread, blessed and broke it, and gave it to his two companions. Immediately, the disciples recognized him. Jesus vanished, and the disciples said, "Weren't our hearts burning while he was opening Scripture to us?" They returned to Jerusalem and told the other disciples what happened.

Number the parts of the Liturgy of the Word in order.

1. _____ The Second Reading / "Thanks be to God."

2. _____ The Creed

3. _____ The Responsorial Psalm

4. _____ The Homily

5. _____ Universal Prayer (Prayer of the Faithful)

6. _____ The Gospel / "Praise to you, Lord Jesus Christ."

7. _____ The First Reading / "Thanks be to God."

8. _____ The Alleluia verse (or, in Lent, usually "Glory and praise to you, Lord Jesus Christ.")

Pay close attention to the next homily you hear. Listen for what it tells you about the Scripture readings.

THE LITURGY OF THE HOURS: THE DIVINE OFFICE

Objective
The children will be able to define the Liturgy of the Hours and know that Scripture is at its core.

Catechist Notes
Jewish people prayed seven times a day. Christians adopted this custom, which evolved into the Liturgy of the Hours. The hours coincide with key events: morning (the resurrection), midmorning (Pentecost), noon (crucifixion and the realization that Gentiles should be accepted into the church), midafternoon (death of Jesus), and evening (Last Supper).

You might form three groups and assign each one a canticle prayed in the Liturgy of the Hours: Mary's (Luke 1:46–55), Zechariah's (Luke 1:68–79), and Simeon's (Luke 2:29–32). After they read it, ask them to share one thought from it with the class.

Materials
- [ ] **ON THE BOARD OR ON POSTER PAPER:**
  APYR   YAAWSL
- [ ] **A COPY OF CHRISTIAN PRAYER** *(optional)*
- [ ] **A RECORDING OF GREGORIAN CHANT** *(optional)*
- [ ] **A CD PLAYER** *(optional)*
- [ ] **COPIES OF ACTIVITY SHEET 17**

Activity
❶ Challenge the children to unscramble the displayed letters to read Paul's message in 1 Thessalonians 5:17. (Pray always.) Ask how we are able to pray always. (Answers will vary.)

❷ Show a copy of *Christian Prayer* if you have one and state:
- The Liturgy of the Hours, the church's official daily prayer, enables us to pray always. Because this prayer is prayed at certain hours each day, it sanctifies the whole day; it makes it holy.

❸ Ask the children what times of day they pray. (morning and night) Write Morning Prayer at the top of the board or poster paper and Night Prayer some distance below it. State that these are two of the hours. Fill in the remaining hours: Midmorning, Midday, Midafternoon, and Evening.

❹ Present the names for the Liturgy of the Hours.
- The Liturgy of the Hours is also called the Divine Office, which means "divine work." Priests pray the Liturgy of the Hours from books called breviaries. Some monastic communities rise during the night and early morning to pray it. They chant the prayers. *[Play a selection of Gregorian chant if you have a recording.]*
- The Liturgy of the Hours is also called the Prayer of Christians because all Christians are intended to pray it.

❺ Explain the structure of the hours.
- The hours are mostly composed of prayers from Scripture. They include psalms, canticles, and the Our Father. There is also a reading from Scripture. Just like at Mass, there are intercessions.
- Additional prayers are related to the feast day or the liturgical season that is being celebrated that day. For example, on March 19, the feast of St. Joseph, the Divine Office ends with a special prayer about him.

❻ Distribute copies of Activity Sheet 17. Assign sides, appoint a leader and a reader, and then pray the midday prayer with the children.

Prayer
God, you give me the gift of life each day. Help me to remember to pray every day, at least in the morning and at night. Then, my days will be holier.

Wednesday Midday Prayer
ABRIDGED

Leader: God, come to my assistance.
All: Lord, make haste to help me.
Leader: Glory to the Father, and to the Son, and to the Holy Spirit.
All: As it was in the beginning, is now and will be forever. Amen.

Leader: Lord, may you be forever blessed; teach me the ways of holiness.

PSALM 119:9–16

Side 1: How shall the young remain sinless?
By obeying your word.
I have sought you with all my heart:
Let me not stray from your commands.

Side 2: I treasure your promise in my heart
Lest I sin against you.
Blessed are you, O Lord;
Teach me your statutes.

Side 1: With my tongue I have recounted
The decrees of your lips.
I rejoiced to do your will
As though all riches were mine.

Side 2: I will ponder all your precepts
And consider your paths.
I take delight in your statutes;
I will not forget your word.

PSALM PRAYER

All: Lord, may we treasure your commandments as the greatest of all riches; never let us fear that anything will be wanting to us while you are at our side.

READING

Reader: Become holy yourselves in every aspect of your conduct, after the likeness of the holy One who called you; remember, Scripture says, "Be holy, for I am holy." (1 Peter 1:15–16)

Leader: May your priests be robed with holiness.
All: Let your people dance for joy.

PRAYER

Leader: God of mercy, this midday moment of rest is your welcome gift. Bless the work we have begun, make good its defects, and let us finish it in a way that pleases you. Grant this through Christ our Lord.

CONCLUSION

Leader: Let us praise the Lord.
All: And give him thanks.

18 HOW TO READ SCRIPTURE

Objective

The children will read the Bible as if it were God's word to them personally, using helps to understand what they read.

Catechist Notes

The Bible is a unique book. As sacred writing, it ought to be read prayerfully and with reverence— as someone said, only on one's knees! Because Scripture is a means to encounter God, it needs to be read listening for what God is saying to us personally. Furthermore, Scripture can only be comprehended correctly by reading it carefully, by being aware of its literary styles and the culture that produced it, and by interpreting it in the context of the whole Bible and Catholic teaching. Hopefully, this lesson will inculcate in children not only a desire to read the Bible but also the attitudes and tools to do so with profit.

You might be able to give the children some quiet time to read the Gospel of Mark independently. This is probably the easiest book for them to understand.

Materials

☐ **BIBLE**
☐ **PIECES OF JUNK MAIL**
☐ **PENS OR PENCILS**
☐ **COPIES OF ACTIVITY SHEET 18**

Activity

❶ Lead the children to see that a love letter is the best kind to receive. Show some junk mail and ask:

- What do people usually do with mail addressed "To Occupant"? (throw it away)
- What is the best kind of letter to receive? (a personal one) Why? (It is about your relationship with someone, experiences you shared.)
- What is the best kind of personal letter? (a love letter)

❷ Discuss how to read a love letter.

- Someday you might receive a love letter. How does a person read a love letter? (slowly, repeating words and phrases, savoring it, reading between the lines, memorizing parts of it)
- This is how we should read the Bible because it is a love letter from God to us.
- God speaks directly to our hearts in Scripture. St. Bernard said that we should read the Bible with the ear of our heart.

❸ State that although the Bible was written thousands of years ago for a people very different from us, it has meaning for us today. Martin Luther said, "The Bible is alive, it speaks to me; it has feet, it runs after me; it has hands, it lays hold on me."

❹ Share a time when Scripture was especially meaningful to you. Ask the children to share such a time.

❺ Distribute copies of Activity Sheet 18. Direct the children to read the sheet independently and decide which tip they think is most important. Discuss their answers and the reasons for them. Then ask which tip they plan to incorporate in their reading of Scripture.

❻ Quote this saying and ask what it means: "A person whose Bible is falling apart usually isn't." (Someone who reads the Bible a lot has a good, happy life.)

Prayer

Speak, Lord, I'm listening.
Let your holy word sink deep into my heart.

Seven Tips for Bible Reading

Read the tips here and in the box check the one you think is most important.
Then circle the tip you would like to follow.

1 Pray to the Holy Spirit before you begin: "Come, Holy Spirit, fill the hearts of your faithful and kindle in them the fire of your love."

2 Believe that God can communicate with you through Scripture. A woman was cured when she had the faith to touch the hem of Jesus' robe secretly. We ought to "touch Christ" in the Bible with the same faith and expectancy.

3 Realize that you won't understand everything. But you can understand more by reading footnotes and Bible commentaries and by joining Bible study groups.

4 Read verses in the context of the whole passage and the whole Bible. For instance, Psalm 14:1 says, "There is no god," but before this are the words, "The fool says in his heart."

5 Pay attention to the literary writing style. For example, don't take fiction literally. The account of Jonah living three days inside a large fish is a story or parable that is intended to teach about God's mercy.

6 Learn about the culture and time of the people who wrote the Bible. For example, Jesus said if our eye sins, pluck it out. This sounds harsh unless you know that Jewish people exaggerated to make a point.

7 Make notes in your Bible. Write comments, highlight, underline, and star words. Or in a special notebook make notes about what you read.

Special advice . . .

KEEP YOUR BIBLE

ON YOUR PILLOW.

EVERY NIGHT

BEFORE YOU GO

TO BED, READ A

COUPLE OF VERSES.

SOME NIGHTS,

YOU MIGHT FIND

YOURSELF READING

EVEN MORE!

PRAYERS IN THE BIBLE

Objective

The children will realize that many of our prayers originated in Scripture.

Catechist Notes

The Bible is the source for many of our prayers. In particular, we made the Jewish Book of Psalms our own. When we pray the psalms, we are praying the prayers that God gave us to pray. We are also praying the prayers that Jesus, Mary, and Joseph prayed. The violence in some psalms may be disturbing, but the Israelites were constantly in battles. They fought for God and looked to God to save them. When we pray these verses, we can consider the "enemies" our sins, diseases, or the Evil One.

Dorothy Day, co-founder of the Catholic Worker Movement, said, "My strength returns to me with my morning cup of coffee and reading the psalms."

Materials

☐ **Bibles**
☐ **Recording of a hymn** *that is Scripture set to music*
☐ **CD player**
☐ **Pens or pencils**
☐ **Copies of Activity Sheet 19**

Activity

❶ Play a hymn based on Scripture, or better, have the children sing one. Announce the Scripture source for the hymn. Comment that many of our hymns and prayers are taken from the Bible.

❷ Ask the children where the following prayers came from.
- Our Father (the gospels)
- Hail Mary (The first part is the Angel Gabriel's words to Mary combined with Elizabeth's words to Mary found in the Gospel of Luke.)
- Psalms (the Old Testament)

❸ Give examples of prayers in the Bible.
- Some prayers in Scripture are canticles—song-prayers. These include Mary's Magnificat (Luke 1:46–55), Zechariah's Benedictus (Luke 1:68–79), and Simeon's Nunc Dimittis (Luke 2:29–32).
- Moses, his sister Miriam, Judith, and other people in the Bible also sang to God.
- The Bible book Song of Songs is one long canticle said to be written by King Solomon.

❹ Introduce the psalms.
- At Mass before the gospel we pray a psalm.
- The Book of Psalms in the Bible is a collection of Jewish song-prayers. It is the longest book.
- The word *psalm* comes from the Greek for "a song sung to a plucked instrument."
- Another name for the Book of Psalms is the Psalter.
- Psalms are prayed in the Liturgy of the Hours. Some people pray psalms privately.
- Many of the hymns we sing are psalms set to music.

❺ Distribute copies of Activity Sheet 19 and give the children time to work them. Then correct their answers. **Answers:** *Part I: 1) David; 2) years; 3) praise; 4) Temple; 5) Jesus; 6) complain; 7) seven; 8) Messiah; 9) wisdom; 10) reigns. Part II. My psalter is my joy.*

❻ Conclude by praying the blessing over the children that is under "Prayer." Inform them that this blessing is found in the Bible.

Prayer

"The Lord bless you and keep you; The Lord make his face to shine upon you, and be gracious to you; The Lord lift up his countenance upon you, and give you peace" (Numbers 6:24–26).

The Psalms: Songs of Praise

≡ PART ONE ≡
Unscramble the missing words and write them on the lines.

1. The psalms are song-prayers said to be composed by King _____.

V I D D A

2. They actually were written over a span of six hundred _____.

S E R Y A

3. These 150 prayers of _____ form the longest book in the Bible.

I E S R A P

4. The Israelites prayed the psalms on the way to and in the _____.

E M L E T P

5. _____ prayed the psalms as did Mary and the apostles.

S S E J U

6. Many psalms are laments in which we _____ to God but trust him.

N A C O M P L I

7. _____ psalms are penitential in which we ask God for forgiveness.

V N E E S

8. Some psalms foretell of a _____ and are quoted in the gospels.

H A M I E S S

9. Psalms is one of the _____ books, for some psalms tell us how to live.

M I S O W D

10. The main theme of the Book of Psalms is "Yahweh _____."

N S R G I E

≡ PART TWO ≡
Write the letter that comes before each given one.

_ _   _ _ _ _ _ _ _ _   _ _
N Z   Q T B M U F S   J T

_ _ _ _ _ .   ST. AUGUSTINE
N Z K P Z

20 MEDITATING USING OUR SENSES

Objective

The children will experience a meditation in which they draw on their senses to make a gospel story come to life.

Catechist Notes

The traditional definition of prayer is "lifting the mind and heart to God." Meditation, or reflecting on God or a holy topic, is one form of mental prayer. St. Ignatius gave us a unique way to meditate on a gospel story. He advised employing all of the senses as we imagine the story taking place. It is as though we are present, part of the scene. This brings the gospel events to life and makes them more vivid and memorable. An extension of this prayer experience would be to rewrite the gospel story in the first person, noting what you see, hear, smell, and so on. Conclude with you and Jesus alone and discussing what occurred. Write your conversation making references to what is going on in your life.

Materials
- ☐ **BIBLE**
- ☐ **PENS OR PENCILS**
- ☐ **BOARD OR POSTER PAPER**
- ☐ **COPIES OF ACTIVITY SHEET 20**

Activity

❶ Write the letters S, H, T, T, S on the board or poster paper and tell the children that they are the initials of our five senses. Ask what these senses are and write each one as children name them: sight, hearing, taste, touch, and smell.

❷ Explain meditating the St. Ignatius way.
- A little boy once said, "Sometimes I think about God even when I'm not praying." This child didn't know that thinking about God is a form of prayer. It is called meditation.
- Today you will meditate on a gospel story in a special way. You will call on your five senses to make the events more real for you.

❸ Read aloud the story of Bartimaeus in Mark 10:46–52.

❹ Distribute copies of Activity Sheet 20. Form groups of three or four and have the children answer the questions together.

❺ When the groups are finished with the activity, read the questions and let the children share their answers with everyone. **POSSIBLE ANSWERS:** *1) many people; talking, birds; stones, hot sun; sweat, dust; 2) ragged, faded; in the dirt, cross-legged; cloudy, closed, staring; 3) shook him; 4) staggering; with help; 5) firm, loving; 6) pleading; 7) radiant, happy; 8) face of Jesus.*

❻ Direct the children to replay the story of Bartimaeus in their minds as though they were watching a television show. Encourage them to fill in the details based on the Activity Sheet. Allow five or ten minutes of quiet time for this.

❼ Conclude the prayer period.
- Bartimaeus flung off his cloak so that nothing would hold him back from Jesus. Think: What might be keeping you from Jesus, such as not praying, skipping Mass, or a bad habit? End your meditation by asking Jesus to help you to come closer to him.

Prayer

"Let the words of my mouth and the meditation of my heart be acceptable to you, O LORD, my rock and my redeemer" (**PSALM 19:14**).

Bartimaeus,

THE BLIND BEGGAR WHO SEES

Answer the questions to help imagine the story of Bartimaeus.

1. If you were walking in the crowd with Jesus in the warm country on the dirt road, what would you see?

_____

Hear?_____

Feel? _____

Smell? _____

2. What were the clothes of Bartimaeus like?

_____

_____

How was he sitting?

_____

What did his blind eyes look like?

_____

3. How did people try to quiet Bartimaeus?

_____

4. How did blind Bartimaeus walk to Jesus?

_____

5. What was the voice of Jesus like when he asked, "What do you want me to do for you?"

_____

6. How did Bartimaeus say, "I want to see"?

_____

7. What did the face of Bartimaeus look like when he realized he could see?

_____

8. What was the first thing Bartimaeus saw?

_____

21 *LECTIO DIVINA,* SACRED READING

Objective
The children will identify the steps in *lectio divina* and experience them.

Catechist Notes
Pope Francis defines *lectio divina* as a "way of listening to what the Lord wishes to tell us in his word and of letting ourselves be transformed by the Spirit." Although *lectio divina* is best used for Scripture, it can also be used when reading other spiritual material. Some people add a fifth step: action.

Materials
- ☐ **A MATH BOOK, COOKBOOK, AND NOVEL**
- ☐ **CANDLE AND MATCHES** (*if fire laws allow*) ·
- ☐ **A PEACEFUL HYMN**
- ☐ **A CD PLAYER**
- ☐ **COPIES OF ACTIVITY SHEET 21**

Activity
❶ Ask the children how they would read a math book? A cookbook? A novel? Conclude that different types of books require different ways of reading.

❷ Explain *lectio divina.*
- Long ago people discovered a special way to read Scripture. This way united them with God dwelling in their hearts. It is called *lectio divina*, which is Latin for "sacred reading."
- *Lectio divina* has four steps.

❸ Distribute copies of Activity Sheet 21. Have the children follow the chart on it as you explain the steps of *lectio divina.*
- Step 1: Read. We read the Bible until a word or phrase grabs our attention.
- Step 2: Reflect. We repeat the word or phrase and ponder why it stood out for us. Eventually we realize why. This is the "aha" moment.
- Step 3: Pray. Understanding what the word or phrase means for us prompts us to respond to God. Our response could be a short prayer of adoration, love, contrition, petition, or intercession.
- Step 4: Contemplate. We silently rest in God's presence, aware that God is within us, loving us. This is the highest form of prayer.
- In the first three steps we are doing something. In the last step we are simply being.
- The first three steps involve words. The last step is wordless.

❹ Lead the children through *lectio divina.* Form groups of four or five. Light a candle (if fire laws allow). Tell the children that the psalm will be read twice and they should listen for a word or phrase that touches their heart. Assure the children that silence is all right. They need not speak.
- Recall that God is present with the children.
- Let each group choose a child to read the psalm on the activity sheet.
- Remind the children to listen for a special word or phrase, and then tell the readers to read the psalm aloud.
- Have another child in each group reread the psalm.
- Invite the children to share with the rest of their group the word or phrase that attracted them.
- Play a quiet hymn.
- Invite the children to pray one sentence aloud that their word or phrase prompts them to pray.
- Let the children remain in silence for a while.

Prayer
"I treasure your word in my heart, so that I may not sin against you" (PSALM 119:11).

Lectio Divina:
A WAY TO GOD

contemplate

Rest in God.

pray

Pray a short act of love, thanks, adoration, contrition, petition, or intercession.

reflect

Think about why the word or phrase has special meaning for you.

read

Read until a word or phrase grabs your attention.

The patriarch Jacob had a vision of a ladder reaching to heaven. Lectio divina is like this ladder.

PSALM 86:1–7

Please listen, LORD
and answer my prayer!
I am poor and helpless.
Protect me and save me
   because you are my God.
I am your faithful servant,
   and I trust you.
Be kind to me!
I pray to you all day.
Make my heart glad!
I serve you,
   and my prayer is sincere.
You willingly forgive,
and your love is always there
   for those who pray to you.

Contemporary English Version

22 MEMORIZING VERSES

Objective
The students will be convinced of the value of memorizing Scripture and know ways to commit verses to memory.

Catechist Notes
Master catechist Janaan Manternach called memorizing Scripture "banking prayers." Verses committed to memory rise to our minds when we need them. When a prayer book isn't handy, they are a springboard for prayer. Long ago, illiterate people, such as the Blessed Virgin Mary, memorized prayers. At one time, the requirement for becoming a monk was knowing all one hundred fifty psalms by heart! Pope John Paul II wrote that "the blossoms of faith and piety...do not grow in the desert places of a memoryless catechesis" (*Catechesis in Our Time*, 55). Children find it easier to memorize than we do.

Materials
☐ **WRITTEN ON AN ERASABLE BOARD:** *"For God so loved the world that he gave his only Son, so that everyone who believes in him may not perish but may have eternal life." (John 3:16)*
☐ **COPIES OF ACTIVITY SHEET 22**

Activity
❶ Ask the children to name something they have memorized and tell how it has helped them. (the ABCs, numbers, their address and phone number)

❷ Develop the value of memorizing Scripture.
- Why is it good to memorize Scripture verses? (This puts God's word in our heart. We could use the verses to pray. When we don't have a Bible, we can still "read" Scripture.)

❸ Help the children memorize John 3:16 by having them read the passage on the board over and over. After each reading, erase a word or two until the children are reciting the entire passage by heart.

❹ Present using Scripture verses as mantras.
- Once you have Scripture verses memorized, they can rise to the surface of your mind as prayer.
- An easy way to pray is to repeat a Scripture verse over and over. This is praying because it fixes our attention on God and makes us aware that God is with us.
- Sometimes we are too tired, too worried, or too sick to pray any other way. But we can always repeat a short line like "The Lord is my shepherd" (Psalm 23:1), "Help me, O Lord my God!" (Psalm 109:26), or "I will give thanks to you, O Lord" (Isaiah 12:1).
- A line repeated in prayer like this is called a mantra. Praying mantras is very comforting.

❺ Distribute copies of Activity Sheet 22. Read the tips for memorizing with the children. Ask them which ones they think would help them most.

❻ Direct the children to choose a verse from the box on the sheet and memorize it, perhaps using one of the ten tips.

❼ After allowing enough time for memory work, let several children recite their chosen verses. Ask each one how they memorized their verse.

Prayer
*Lord, you say to me, "My child, keep my words, and store up my commandments with you. Write them on the tablet of your heart" (**PROVERBS 7:1, 3**).*
May I learn many of your precious words by heart.

Ten Tips for Memorizing Scripture Verses

1. Think about what the verse means. Look up unfamiliar words in a dictionary or on the Internet.

2. Recite the verse aloud over and over.

3. Write the verse several times.

4. Display the verse where you will see it: your desk or dresser, a mirror, or the refrigerator.

5. Make a jigsaw puzzle out of the words and work it over and over. For fun, make two copies and race with someone in putting the puzzle together.

6. Make up motions to do as you say the verse.

7. Sing the verse to a tune.

8. For a long verse, memorize one section at a time.

9. Memorize a verse while traveling, exercising, or waiting for something. Memorize a verse right before you go to bed. It sticks better.

10. Set a goal, such as: I will master this in fifteen minutes.

TO LEARN BY HEART . . .

The LORD is my shepherd, I shall not want. He makes me lie down in green pastures; he leads me beside still waters; he restores my soul. He leads me in right paths for his name's sake. (PSALM 23:1-3)

Do not fear, for I have redeemed you; I have called you by name, you are mine. When you pass through the waters, I will be with you; and through the rivers, they shall not overwhelm you; when you walk through fire you shall not be burned. (ISAIAH 43:1-2)

You are the light of the world. A city built on a hill cannot be hid. In the same way, let your light shine before others, so that they may see your good works and give glory to your Father in heaven. (MATTHEW 5:14, 16)

Store up for yourselves treasures in heaven, where neither moth nor rust consumes and where thieves do not break in and steal. For where your treasure is, there your heart will be also. (MATTHEW 6:20-21)

Just as I have loved you, you also should love one another. By this everyone will know that you are my disciples, if you have love for one another. (JOHN 13:34B-35)

23 BIBLE REFERENCE BOOKS

Objective
The children will become familiar with references that help us read and understand Scripture.

Catechist Notes
The Second Vatican Council's "Dogmatic Constitution on Divine Revelation" encourages catechists to "hold fast to the sacred Scriptures through diligent sacred reading and careful study" (25). Then by being a listener to it inwardly, they will not be an empty preacher of the word of God outwardly. You will help your children listen to Scripture inwardly by introducing them to the many tools available for breaking open God's word. You might see to it that your church and school libraries are equipped with these reference books. Notably, Mark Twain commented that it wasn't the parts of the Bible he didn't understand that bothered him, but those he did understand!

Materials
☐ **Bible reference books, such as a concordance, a study Bible, a Bible dictionary, a Bible atlas, a Bible commentary**
☐ **An ordo**
☐ **A lectionary**
☐ **Copies of Activity Sheet 23**

Activity
❶ Talk about reference books.
- In the library are special books called reference books. Usually we only refer to them for information in the library. We can't check them out. What are some of these? (dictionary, atlas, encyclopedia)
- Some reference books give information about the Bible that helps us understand it. Today a play will introduce you to them.

❷ Distribute copies of Activity Sheet 23. Assign parts for the play: Narrator, Mrs. Drew, Tom, Susan, and Bob. Have the chosen children read the play.

❸ Review the biblical reference books.
- What book lists all the verses that contain a certain word? (concordance)
- What book gives us lengthy explanations of biblical words? (biblical encyclopedia)
- What book has maps of the lands referred to in the Bible? (biblical atlas)
- What book contains definitions of people, places, and things in the Bible? (biblical dictionary)
- What book tells how to say biblical names and words? (pronunciation guide)
- What book contains the Bible along with explanations of passages? (study Bible)
- What book offers explanations of the Bible's verses? (Bible commentary)
- What book tells about the people in the Bible? (Bible who's who)

❹ State that there two more books related to the Bible. Show the lectionary and the ordo and explain:
- A lectionary contains all the readings for the Masses. The lector at Mass reads from it.
- An ordo is a small book that lists the readings for each day's Mass.

❺ From each book you brought, give an example of a piece of information it provides.

❻ Let the children browse through the books you brought.

Prayer
O God, your word is rich in meaning for me. I want to learn more about it and be at home in it. Help me use the tools that will enable me to tap into Scripture. That way I will also learn more about you.

Helps for Bible Reading: A Play

> ★ **CAST:** Narrator, Mrs. Drew, Tom, Susan, and Bob

Narrator: In religion class Tom, Bob, and Susan were assigned to report on King Solomon. They go to the school librarian, Mrs. Drew, for help.

Tom: Mrs. Drew, we're making a report on King Solomon. Where should we start looking for information?

Mrs. Drew: Here are two books that will help you. A Bible encyclopedia has long explanations of people, places, and things in the Bible. A Bible who's who tells about the people in the Bible.

Narrator: The children read the entries for King Solomon and take notes.

Susan: Mrs. Drew, where in the world is King Solomon's kingdom, Israel?

Mrs. Drew: Here is a Bible atlas. You can find maps of Israel and its neighboring countries in here. Or you can locate it on a globe.

Bob: The Bible encyclopedia said that in the Temple, Solomon placed the ark of the covenant. What is that?

Mrs. Drew: A Bible dictionary will tell you what the ark is. Where do you think you would find a longer explanation?

Susan: I know! A Bible encyclopedia.

Bob: By the way, we have to read our report to the class. Solomon had a large fleet in the Gulf of A-q-a-b-a. How do you say that?

Mrs. Drew: A pronunciation guide to biblical terms will answer that.

Tom: I'd like to read all of the passages in the Bible about Solomon, but how will I find them?

Mrs. Drew: There is a fantastic book called a concordance. It has thousands of words. Under each word is a list of all the verses in the Bible that include that word.

Tom: Wow! I feel sorry for the person who had to put that together.

Bob: My problem is that when I read the Bible, I don't understand some of the verses.

Mrs. Drew: In that case, you might consult a Bible commentary. It explains the verses. There are also versions of the Bible called study Bibles that do the same thing.

Susan: I bet we could find out all about King Solomon on the Internet.

Mrs. Drew: You're right, Susan. Websites like Biblestudytool.com can be a big help. Happy hunting!

24 GOSPELS: THE HEART OF THE BIBLE

Objective
The children will view the gospels as the heart of the Bible and name characteristics of each one.

Catechist Notes
Many gospels were circulating in the early church. Four were chosen for the canon because of their apostolic origin and use in liturgy.

Materials
- ☐ **BIBLES**
- ☐ **PENS OR PENCILS**
- ☐ **FLASHCARDS: MATTHEW, MARK, LUKE, JOHN**
- ☐ **COPIES OF ACTIVITY SHEET 24**

Activity
❶ Instruct the children to think of someone they know. Ask:
- If you were going to write the story of this person's life, what would you include? (What the person did and said, their personality, their likes and dislikes, their jobs, their relatives)
- Your written account would not be exactly like someone else's story about this person. Why not? (We would each have our own view of him or her.)

❷ Present the four gospels.
- The apostles told stories about Jesus. People started writing these stories down. Some accounts were called gospels, which means "telling good news."
- Each gospel presented a different view of Jesus. They were like different portraits. The view depended on the audience the writer was targeting, for example, Jews or Gentiles.
- The church chose four gospels to include in the Bible: the gospels of Matthew, Mark, Luke, and John.

- The gospel writers are called evangelists. This word comes from the Greek word for good news.
- We think Mark's gospel was written first. John's gospel was written last.
- Because the gospels are about Jesus, they are the heart of the Bible. When a gospel is read at Mass, we stand out of respect for Jesus.

❸ Distribute the copies of Activity Sheet 24. Direct the children to complete the worksheet. When they are finished, let them share their answers.

❹ Review the gospels by a game. Form four groups and give each a flashcard with a gospel name. Station each group in a corner of the room. Ask a question and have the group with the answer say it. What gospel . . .
- was the first one written? (Mark)
- is the most theological? It presents Jesus as Son of God. (John)
- was written for Jewish Christians and so refers to many Old Testament prophecies? (Matthew)
- focuses on salvation for everyone? (Luke)
- was the last gospel written? (John)
- has "I am" sayings of Jesus that identify him with God? (John)
- has most of the stories about Jesus' birth? (Luke)
- is often called the gospel of women? (Luke)
- has five long sermons? (Matthew)
- is poetic and reflective? (John)
- has the most details and is most historical? (Mark)

Prayer
Jesus, by pondering your words and actions in the gospels, may I come to love you more and be eager to share the gospel.

The Gospels
FOUR PORTRAITS OF JESUS

Read about each gospel and skim it to look for what you are to find. Study this sheet.

GOSPEL OF
MARK

- Mark's gospel focuses on the suffering Christ.

- Written for Gentile converts in Rome, it encouraged persecuted Christians.

- This gospel is the most historical.

- The book is fast moving with many details.

Find two verses that contain the words "immediately" or "at once." Write their citations here:

_____

_____

GOSPEL OF
MATTHEW

- Written for Jewish converts, this gospel has many Old Testament quotations.

- It shows how Jesus fulfills prophecies.

- It presents Jesus as the Messiah and the new Moses.

- The gospel contains five sermons.

- It often speaks of the kingdom of heaven.

Find one Old Testament prophecy this gospel refers to. Write its citation here:

_____

GOSPEL OF
LUKE

- Luke, a Greek doctor, wrote for Greek Gentiles.

- A message of this gospel is that salvation is for everyone.

- Most of the stories about the birth and early life of Jesus are in the Gospel of Luke.

- This gospel is known as the gospel of prayer, forgiveness, pardon, joy, the Holy Spirit, and women.

Find three stories in Luke that feature women. Write their citations here:

_____

_____

_____

GOSPEL OF
JOHN

- John's gospel stresses the divinity of Jesus, the Son of God.

- God revealed to Moses that his name was "I am who am." In John's gospel, Jesus often states, "I am," such as "I am the light" and "I am the good shepherd."

- This gospel is very poetic and reflective.

- It contains long discourses (speeches) of Jesus, like the one at the Last Supper.

- The gospel presents the sacraments in stories.

Find one story that is related to baptism, the Eucharist, reconciliation, or matrimony. Write its citation here:

_____

 The first three gospels are similar. They are called the synoptic gospels. *Synoptic* **means "same view."**

25 HEBREW POETRY

Objective

The children will know some features of Hebrew poetry and identify them in a few Scripture passages.

Catechist Notes

Poetry is found throughout Scripture, from the opening lines of Genesis to the songs in Revelation. Obviously the Book of Psalms contains the most well-known biblical poetry. Some scriptural poems, like Miriam's song in Exodus 15:21, have ancient roots. Some passages in the New Testament appear to be early Christian hymns—for example, Philippians 2:5–11. While Hebrew poetry shares some characteristics with our poetry, it has some unique ones. Teaching your children to be attuned to the features of Hebrew poetry will heighten their understanding and appreciation of it.

If time allows, you might challenge your students to comb the psalms for other examples of the characteristics of poetry. You also might have them compose an acrostic prayer-poem using the letters of their name.

Materials

- ☐ **BIBLES**
- ☐ **PENS OR PENCILS**
- ☐ **A HYMN THAT IS A PSALM WITH A MUSICAL SETTING**, *such as Psalm 23*
- ☐ **CD PLAYER**
- ☐ **COPIES OF ACTIVITY SHEET 25**

Activity

❶ Recite "Roses are red; violets are blue. Sugar is sweet, and so are you." Ask what makes this a poem. (rhythm, rhyme, a comparison: sugar and the loved one)

❷ Introduce Hebrew poetry.

- ■ Poetry in the Bible has these characteristics too. However, most of the poems were written in Hebrew, and we have an English translation. As a result, the rhythm and rhyme in the original poems are hidden from us.
- ■ However, Hebrew poetry is filled with comparisons that do carry over into our language. In English class you probably learned about metaphors and similes. What is the difference? (A simile is a comparison that uses like or as; a metaphor is a comparison that lacks these words.) Who can give an example of a metaphor? A simile?
- ■ Today a worksheet will guide you through these and other characteristics of Hebrew poetry. That way, when you pray a psalm, like the responsorial psalm at Mass, you will appreciate it more.

❸ Distribute copies of Activity Sheet 25. Work the sheet together with the class, or have the children work it independently. **ANSWERS:** *1) "For his steadfast love endures forever." Word, God, being, life, light, darkness; 2) my foes; 3) rock, sheep; 4) a lonely bird on the housetop; 5) collecting our tears in a bottle; knitting us in our mother's womb; 6) decrees, precepts, statutes, commandments, ordinances, statutes; 7) clap their hands.*

❹ State that many of our hymns are based on the psalms and other poetry in the Bible. Direct the children to locate the psalm in the Bible that matches your chosen hymn. Have them read the verses used in the song. Then play the hymn, having the children sing along if possible.

Prayer

"O sing to the LORD a new song, for he has done marvelous things" (PSALM 98:1).

Plunging into Poetry

Use your Bible to answer the questions.

1. Hebrew poetry repeats words. What words appear in every verse of Psalm 136?

_____

In John 1:1–5, what words are repeated? _____

2. Ideas are also repeated. A second line echoes the first with the same or similar words. In Psalm 3:1 what is the same as those "rising against me"?

_____

3. Metaphors are comparisons. In Psalm 95:1 what is God compared to?

_____

In Psalm 95:7, what are we compared to? _____

4. Similes are comparisons that use like or as. In Psalm 102:7 to what does the sad psalmist compare himself?

_____

5. Hebrew poetry has vivid imagery. What does Psalm 56:8 picture God doing?

_____

What does Psalm 139:13 picture God doing? _____

6. Some psalms are acrostic. Each verse begins with a consecutive letter of the Hebrew alphabet, which has twenty-two letters. In Psalm 119 each of these letters in order has eight verses that begin with it. What's more, each of the 176 verses contains a synonym for God's law. In verses 2–8 what are these synonyms?

_____

7. In poetry things may have human characteristics. In Isaiah 55:12 what do trees do?

_____

26 KNOWING THE CULTURE

Objective
The children will realize the importance of understanding the cultures at the times the Bible was written.

Catechist Notes
Not knowing about the times of the biblical authors, we might be puzzled by or misunderstand Bible passages—even miss the point entirely! The more we know about the food, clothing, customs, and religion of the Old Testament Jewish people, the more we will understand their stories. Likewise, the more we know about the culture in New Testament times, the more we will understand Jesus and his messages. Archaeologists and historians constantly uncover new facts about biblical times. You might share a recent discovery with your children.

Materials
☐ **Pens or pencils**
☐ **Copies of Activity Sheet 26**

Activity
❶ Tell the children to suppose that an alien from another planet visited their country. Ask what the alien would need to know to understand them, their newspapers, and television programs. (the language, the customs, the government, the food, clothing, etiquette, attitudes, and so forth)

❷ Explain the importance of knowing the Jewish culture.

■ A people's way of life is called its culture. Our culture is different from the culture of the people in New Guinea or China. Even gestures have different meanings. For example, in some countries a thumbs-up gesture is considered crude. In Russia, giving someone an even number of flowers is like wishing them dead.

■ The people in the Bible lived some two to four thousand years ago. They lived on the other side of the world. Imagine how very different their culture was from ours!

■ To understand some of the Bible stories and passages, it is necessary to know certain things about the Jewish culture. The more we know the culture, the more we know Scripture. And St. Jerome once said that ignorance of Scripture is ignorance of Jesus.

❸ Offer two examples of Jewish customs that impact our understanding of the gospel.

■ The religious leaders were upset that Jesus and the apostles didn't wash their hands before eating. This is because the Jews had a strict custom of performing ceremonial hand washing before meals.

■ Jesus called the Pharisees whitewashed tombs. The Jewish people painted tombs white so that people would see them and not become accidentally unclean by touching them. Being unclean meant you couldn't worship at the Temple until you underwent special washings or offered sacrifice.

❹ Distribute copies of Activity Sheet 26. Direct the children to work them. When they are finished, correct the answers. **Answers:** *1) C; 2) H; 3) J; 4) F; 5) A; 6) I; 7) B; 8) G; 9) D; 10) E.*

Prayer
God, you told Joshua to meditate on the book of the law day and night and to follow all that was written in it (JOSHUA 1:8). You say the same to us today. Help me increase my knowledge of the Hebrew culture so that I may delve deeper into the riches of your word.

The Life and Times of the Hebrews

For each question, write the letter of the correct answer on the line.

QUESTIONS

☐ **1.** Why do many psalms speak about God crushing enemies?

☐ **2.** Why were the religious leaders angry at Jesus for eating with tax collectors?

☐ **3.** Why did everyone go to the Temple in Jerusalem for major feasts?

☐ **4.** Why did King Solomon have so many wives?

☐ **5.** Why was it extraordinary that Jesus touched a leper?

☐ **6.** Why were the apostles surprised that Jesus spoke to the woman at the well?

☐ **7.** Why was it shocking that in a parable Jesus told, the hero was a Samaritan?

☐ **8.** Why did Pilate have "Jesus, King of the Jews" placed above him on the cross?

☐ **9.** When Jesus appeared to the apostles on the day he rose, why did he ask for something to eat?

☐ **10.** Why was the statement of Jesus that a light shouldn't be put under a bed humorous?

ANSWERS

A. Jewish law forbade touching lepers.

B. The Samaritans and the Jews were enemies. Jews avoided passing through Samaria.

C. The Israelites lived in violent times. Tribes and nations were constantly fighting.

D. The Jewish people believed that ghosts do not eat. Jesus was showing that he was really alive.

E. The Jewish people slept on mats, and their lights were oil lamps.

F. At that time, having more than one wife was acceptable, just as it is in some cultures today.

G. The Romans posted the crimes above the heads of criminals.

H. Rome occupied Israel. Tax collectors worked for Rome, the enemy, and sometimes they overcharged people.

I. Jewish men did not speak to women in public.

J. The Temple was the only place where sacrifices were made. It was the center of worship.

27 BIBLE LANDS

Objective

The children will become familiar with the land of Israel and its neighbors.

Catechist Notes

The Bible stories will have a different dimension when the children can visualize the countries that are involved. Learning the modern names for the lands mentioned in the Bible should prove to be interesting for them. Abraham's story, for example, begins in Iraq (Ur) and takes him to Syria (Haran) before God sends him to Israel (Canaan). The Holy Land, Israel, is often called the "fifth gospel" because visiting it, even virtually, brings the gospel stories to life. You might have the children take a virtual tour on a website such as the one found at www.holylandsite.com.

Materials

☐ **A GLOBE OR WORLD MAP**
☐ **PENS OR PENCILS**
☐ **CRAYONS OR MARKERS**
☐ **FLASHCARDS**: *N, S, E, W, Jordan River, Israel, Samaria, Judah, Sea of Galilee, Egypt, Nazareth, Capernaum, Bethlehem, Jerusalem, Mediterranean Sea*
☐ **COPIES OF ACTIVITY SHEET 27**

Activity

❶ Call on a volunteer to locate Israel on a globe or world map. Comment:

■ The Bible lands are in the Middle East. Today some of them have different names. They are often in the news. Abraham lived in what is now Iraq. Then he moved to what is now Syria before going to Israel, which used to be Canaan.

■ We call Israel the Holy Land because that is where Jesus, the Son of God, lived. It is also the promised land God gave to Abraham and the land Moses led the Israelites to from Egypt. Israel was where the Jewish Temple stood.

❷ Share some information about Israel.

■ Israel has hot, dry summers and cool, rainy winters.

■ The Sea of Galilee in the north has been called the most beautiful sea in the world. Fishing was a main industry along its shores. The Jordan River flows from the Sea of Galilee to the Dead Sea in the south. The Dead Sea has no outlet. Because it is filled with salt and other minerals, nothing can live in it.

❸ Distribute copies of Activity Sheet 27. Guide the children in completing the map of Palestine.

■ Israel was divided into three provinces: Galilee in the north, Judah in the south, and Samaria between them. Write their names on the unlettered lines. You can remember their order by thinking "God Sent Jesus." The words' initials (GSJ) are the provinces' initials.

■ Fill in the rest of the map using the given letters as clues. The dots stand for towns.

❹ Reinforce the geography of the Holy Land. Distribute the flashcards to children. Direct those with the N, S, E, and W cards to stand at the north, south, east, and west walls of the room. Instruct the children holding the other cards to stand where they belong in relation to the directions and the other cards.

Prayer

Lord, my land is holy land too because you came to our planet. The ground I walk on, the air I breathe, and the water I drink have all been blessed by your presence. Help me to show reverence for the corner of creation you entrusted to me.

Map Fun

Finish labeling the features on the map of Palestine using the words in the box.
Then lightly color the map.

Judah

Jordan River

Nazareth

Samaria

Jerusalem

Mediterranean
Sea

Galilee

Sea of Galilee

Capernaum

Bethlehem

Dead Sea

The
Holy
Land

M _____
_____

C _____

S____
____

N_____

J____
____

J_____

B_____

D____
____

28 THE BIBLE'S INFLUENCE ON CULTURE

Objective
The children will realize that the Bible has made a great impact on the world's art, music, literature, language, and morals.

Catechist Notes
The themes, characters, and events in the Bible permeate Western culture. We have inherited the Jewish people's monotheism. Our moral code flows from their ten commandments and the laws of Jesus. Much of our music, art, and literature is linked to biblical events and themes. Only those familiar with the Bible will be sensitive to and understand allusions to it. By teaching our children the extent that the Bible is deeply ingrained in who we are, we highlight the Bible's importance. We also convey how necessary it is to be knowledgeable about Scripture.

Materials
- [ ] BIBLES
- [ ] PENS OR PENCILS
- [ ] RECORDING OF HANDEL'S *MESSIAH* OR A SONG FROM A BIBLICAL MUSICAL LIKE *GODSPELL*
- [ ] CD PLAYER
- [ ] PRINTS OF ARTWORK PORTRAYING BIBLICAL SCENES OR A COMPUTER
- [ ] COPIES OF ACTIVITY SHEET 28

Activity
❶ Ask which children have the name of someone in the Bible. (Mary, Matthew, Sarah, Peter, Rachel, John, Luke, and so forth) Comment:
- Many parents give their children biblical names.
- In our country many towns have biblical names. For example, Bethlehem and Eden are in Pennsylvania, Joshua and Palestine are in Texas, and Carmel and Paradise are in California.

❷ Lead the children to see the ways that the Bible has influenced our culture.
- The Bible has influenced us in more ways than providing names. Our culture's morals and attitudes are founded on the Bible. The ten commandments and the teachings of Jesus are the backbone of our justice system.
- Much of our art, music, and literature is based on the Bible. In Shakespeare's plays there are at least twelve hundred references to the Bible.
- Even some of our words and expressions can be traced back to the Bible. For example, where did our expression "a good Samaritan" come from? (a parable Jesus told)

❸ State that it is assumed that an educated person has knowledge of the Bible. Point out that knowing the Bible helps on the quiz show Jeopardy and in working crossword puzzles.

❹ Distribute copies of Activity Sheet 28 and direct the children to complete it.

❺ Discuss the children's answers for numbers 1 through 4. In conjunction with number 1 or 2, play excerpts from the music. With number 4 show biblical artwork, either prints or from the Internet. Then check the answers for number 5. **ANSWERS:** *1) G; 2) A; 3) J; 4) B; 5) D; 6) I; 7) F; 8) C; 9) E; 10) H.*

Prayer
God, in the letter of James you tell us to be doers of the word, and not merely hearers (JAMES 1:22). Please keep me from being an expert in the Bible but a failure in living according to your word.

The Bible Lives On

1. Classical Music. Check the music that you have heard of.

☐ *Elijah* by Felix Mendelssohn

☐ *St. Matthew's Passion* by Johann Sebastian Bach

☐ *Chichester Psalms* by Leonard Bernstein

☐ The opera *Samson and Delilah* by Camille Saint-Saens

☐ *The Messiah* by George Frideric Handel

2. Musicals. Check the musicals that you have seen.

☐ *Joseph and the Amazing Technicolor Dreamcoat*

☐ *Godspell*

☐ *Jesus Christ Superstar*

☐ *Tetelestai*

3. Films. Name some biblical movies:

_____

_____

_____

4. Artwork. Check the artwork you are familiar with.

☐ Michelangelo's *Pietà*

☐ Michelangelo's *Creation of Adam* in the Sistine Chapel

☐ Leonard da Vinci's *Last Supper*

☐ Rembrandt's *The Return of the Prodigal Son*

☐ Fra Angelico's *The Annunciation*

☐ An icon of *Christ Pantocrator*

5. Language. We inherited expressions from the Bible. Look up each Scripture citation, and on the line before it write the letter of the expression found in it.

1. _____ JOB 19:20

2. _____ MATTHEW 15:14

3. _____ JEREMIAH 13:23

4. _____ DEUTERONOMY 32:10

5. _____ GENESIS 4:9

6. _____ ISAIAH 6:5

7. _____ ISAIAH 40:15

8. _____ EXODUS 21:24

9. _____ DANIEL 5:5

10. _____ MATTHEW 7:15

A. The blind leading the blind

B. Apple of his eye

C. Eye for an eye

D. My brother's keeper

E. Handwriting on the wall

F. Drop in the bucket

G. Skin of my teeth

H. Wolves in sheep's clothing

I. Woe is me!

J. Can a leopard change its spots?

29 VERSIONS OF THE BIBLE

Objective
The children will become acquainted with several versions of the Bible and how they differ.

Catechist Notes
Bible translations can be word-for-word (formal equivalence), or they can express thoughts as the new language would convey them (dynamic equivalence). Both methods have their pros and cons.

If you wish to have the children compare more parallel verses than the one on the Activity Sheet, pass out different versions of Bibles. Name Scripture citations and have children read the respective verses. Or go to www.biblestudytools.com where a Scripture citation can be read in different Bibles.

Materials
- ☐ **PAPER**
- ☐ **PENS OR PENCILS**
- ☐ **SEVERAL VERSIONS OF THE BIBLE**, *such as* The New American, The Good News, King James, New Revised Standard Version, *and* The Message
- ☐ **SMALL PRIZE** (optional)
- ☐ **COPIES OF ACTIVITY SHEET 29**

Activity
1. State that the Bible was originally written in Hebrew and Greek. Ask the children to guess how many languages it has been translated into. (about 2,800) You might award a prize to the child who comes closest. Comment that today the children will learn about some English versions of Bibles.

2. Present the difficulty of translating.
   - The written Hebrew language is difficult to translate because it has no vowels and no punctuation. Write your full name this way to see what it would look like.
   - What else makes translating the original languages difficult? (The meanings of some words have changed. Expressions are different.) What are some expressions we use that would puzzle someone not familiar with English? ("You spilled the beans." "He's pulling your leg.")
   - Even though Shakespeare wrote in English, because he lived so long ago, it is sometimes hard for us to understand his plays today. So imagine what it is like figuring out writing from thousands of years ago and in a totally different language.
   - Historians and archaeologists make discoveries about the time period when the Bible was written. These give Scripture scholars insights into the Hebrew and Greek languages of the Bible.

3. Explain the two methods of translating the Bible.
   - Some translators translate the original languages in the Bible literally, that is, word for word. For example, if the words are "His new car was a lemon," that is what they write.
   - Other translators express the idea behind the words. They would write, "His new car had many defects."
   - What kind of Bible do you think is better, one with a literal translation or one that has ideas translated? Why?

4. Distribute copies of Activity Sheet 29. Direct the children to read the descriptions of the Bibles. Tell them to find out what Bible they have at home. Then have them read the translations of Romans 8:28 and give examples of how they differ.

Prayer
The Bible says, "There is no chaining the word of God" (2 TIMOTHY 2:9). O God, may your holy word spread freely throughout the whole world. May more and more people learn of your great love and promise of eternal life.

Bibles to Know About

The Vulgate is St. Jerome's translation of the Bible into Latin. He wrote it in the late fourth century when Latin was the language people spoke. The Vulgate was the first major book printed on Gutenberg's printing press in the 1450s. In the sixteenth century, the Vulgate was named the official Roman Catholic Bible.

Here are Bibles in English along with their translations of Romans 8:28. You can find more Bibles at www.Biblestudytools.com.

KING JAMES BIBLE. An Anglican version from 1611 that is still the most popular Bible among Protestants. Its dignified language includes "thou," "thy," and "-eth," as in "maketh." It lacks the "Catholic" books.	*And we know that all things work together for good to them that love God, to them who are the called according to his purpose.*
THE DOUAY-RHEIMS BIBLE. A translation from the Latin Vulgate published over the late 17th and early 18th centuries. It was the first official Catholic Bible in English.	*And we know that to them that love God all things work together unto good: to such as, according to his purpose, are called to be saints.*
THE JERUSALEM BIBLE. A Bible published in 1966 and revised in 1985 as the *New Jerusalem Bible*. It was the first widely accepted Catholic Bible since the 17th century.	*We know that by turning everything to their good God co-operates with all those who love him, with all those that he has called according to his purpose.*
THE NEW AMERICAN BIBLE. A translation originally published in 1970 and later revised. It is the version that appears in the Lectionary for Mass.	*We know that all things work for good for those who love God, who are called according to his purpose.*
THE NEW REVISED STANDARD VERSION. A translation released in 1989 and approved by Protestants and Catholics.	*We know that all things work together for good for those who love God, who are called according to his purpose.*
THE GOOD NEWS BIBLE. A readable translation by the American Bible Society. The New Testament was published in 1966, and the Old Testament in 1976.	*We know that in all things God works for good with those who love him, those whom he has called according to his purpose.*
THE MESSAGE. A popular translation in contemporary American English that is very understandable.	*That's why we can be so sure that every detail in our lives of love for God is worked into something good.*

30 TIMES THE BIBLE SPEAKS TO US

Objective

The children will realize that in the Bible, God can speak to them in times of need.

Catechist Notes

At times as we read Scripture or hear it proclaimed, it seems as though God were speaking directly to our heart. The words are so pertinent to a current situation we are in that it has to be God at work in us. The prophet Jeremiah claimed this experience was like lightning striking him. We can make use of God's gift of the Bible by going to it for advice, comfort, or confirmation. When we approach Scripture with faith, God doesn't fail us.

Sometimes opening the Bible at random is a way to hear God. When Thomas Merton was debating whether or not to join the Trappists, the order that kept strict silence, he opened a Bible and read, "Be silent," from Psalm 46:10. This method, sometimes called the lucky dip or Bible roulette, is not always dependable. Pondering verses that are known to be related to our needs is safer.

Materials

- ☐ **BIBLES**
- ☐ **A GREETING CARD WITH A SCRIPTURE VERSE**
- ☐ **CARDS POSTCARD SIZE OR LARGER,** *one per child*
- ☐ **PAINT, CRAYONS, OR FELT-TIPPED PENS**
- ☐ **COPIES OF ACTIVITY SHEET 30**

Activity

❶ Show a greeting card with a Scripture verse and read it. Comment:

- Some cards for special occasions contain Scripture verses that correspond to the occasion. For example, a sympathy card might include the verse "Very truly I tell you, whoever believes has eternal life" (John 6:47).
- Through the Bible God can speak to us

during critical times in our lives. He can give us advice when we don't know what to do, and comfort us when are sad, and strengthen us when we are fearful. In the Bible, God also provides words to express our love of him and our joy.

❷ Explain two ways to read the Bible.

- St. Francis of Assisi used his Bible to plan the rules for his religious community. Three times he opened the Bible and read the words his eyes fell upon. In this way he found the three main rules for the Franciscans. He called this method the "first opening."
- Another way to hear God speaking in the Bible is to read verses that we know are related to what we are going through at a particular time.

❸ Distribute copies of Activity Sheet 30 and point out that the verses are appropriate at certain times. Direct the children to look up a few verses and read them aloud.

❹ Pass out art materials. Instruct the children to choose a Scripture verse they like from the activity sheet. Then have them create a card with that verse to display at home.

❺ Encourage the children to keep the activity sheet as a reference for their prayer times.

Prayer

The psalmist says to us, "O that today you would listen to his voice" (PSALM 95:7). Lord, grant me the grace to seek your words for me in Scripture. Then open my ears to listen to them and open my heart to follow them.

Scripture Verses for Special Times

Choose one of the verses. Write it on a card and add decorations around it.
Display the card at home. Keep this sheet where you can refer to it when you need it.

WHAT TO PRAY WHEN YOU ARE . . .

Adoring
Psalm 34:3
Psalm 69:30
Psalm 71:23
Psalm 103:1–2
Revelation 7:12

Afraid
Psalm 27
Psalm 56:3–4
Isaiah 41:10
Philippians 4:6–7
Luke 12:32
John 14:27

Discouraged
Psalm 23:1
Psalm 42:11
Psalm 55:22
1 Corinthians 15:58
Jeremiah 29:11

Happy
Psalm 117
Psalm 150
Luke 1:47
Philippians 4:4

In a Crisis
Psalm 121:7–8
Hebrews 4:16
Psalm 23:4

In Need of Strength
Philippians 4:13
Psalm 28:8
Isaiah 40:31

In Suffering and Pain
Psalm 38:21–22
2 Corinthians 12:9
1 Peter 4:13

In Trouble
Psalm 16:1
Psalm 31:24
Psalm 46:1

Needing Protection
Psalm 27:1
Psalm 91:14

Needing Guidance
Psalm 32:8
Proverbs 3:5

Repentant
Psalm 32:5
Psalm 79:9
1 John 1:9

Sad
Psalm 43:5
John 14:1
Matthew 5:4
Romans 8:38–39
Revelation 21:3–4

Sick
Exodus 15:26
Proverbs 17:22
James 5:15

Tempted
Psalm 1:6
Matthew 26:41
Galatians 6:9

Thankful
Psalm 100:4–5
1 Chronicles 16:34
1 Thessalonians 5:18

Tired
Matthew 11:28
1 Corinthians 2:9

Worried
Philippians 4:6
Matthew 6:25
John 14:1
1 Peter 5:7

OTHER TITLES
IN THIS SERIES

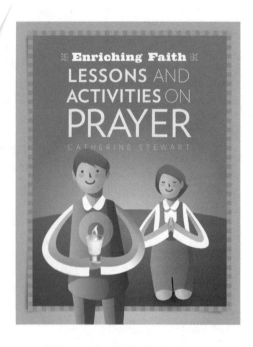

Enriching Faith
Lessons and Activities on Prayer
CATHERINE STEWART

Here are dozens of fresh ideas to help your students see prayer in a whole new light. Easy-to-do activities like the bouncing Prayer Ball, Gratitude Grab Bags, and Spoons of Thankfulness can help you teach traditional, spontaneous, creative and even meditative prayer. Complete with directions, templates, discussion starters, parent letters, catechetical information, and much more.

72 PAGES | $14.95 | 9781585959471

Enriching Faith
Prayers and Activities on Service
PATRICIA MATHSON

Help children make Christian service a way of life with this creative collection of outreach projects, hands-on learning experiences, and joyful prayers. Each activity speaks to children's hearts and includes easy instructions, curriculum connections, and more. Perfect for parish, school, or home-based programs, and anyone who wants to help children become caring and compassionate followers of Christ.

72 PAGES | $14.95 | 9781585959372

1-800-321-0411
23rdpublications.com

TWENTY THIRD 23rd PUBLICATIONS